HENRY V

HENRY V

William Shakespeare

WORDSWORTH CLASSICS

The paper in this book is produced from pure wood
pulp, without the use of chlorine or any other substance
harmful to the environment. The energy used in its
production consists almost entirely of hydroelectricity
and heat generated from waste materials, thereby
conserving fossil fuels and contributing little to the
greenhouse effect.

This edition published 1994 by
Wordsworth Editions Limited
Cumberland House, Crib Street, Ware,
Hertfordshire SG12 9ET

ISBN 1 85326 088 6

Printed and bound by Clays Ltd, St Ives PLC
Typeset in the UK by The R & B Partnership

INTRODUCTION

SHAKESPEARE'S FIRST ATTEMPTS at historical drama may be seen in the tetralogy which comprises the three parts of *Henry VI* and *Richard III*, written between 1590 and 1593. Although it is clear that he had mastered the form in *Richard III*, Shakespeare did not return to history plays until about 1596 with *Richard II; Henry IV* parts one and two followed in about 1597 and this great series was completed in 1599 with *Henry V*.

The first act rehearses the reasons for the King's quarrel with France, presaged in the final scenes of *Henry IV* part two. The Archbishop of Canterbury and the Bishop of Ely confirm the legality of Henry's claim to the throne of France, and when the French Ambassador brings an insulting message to Henry, he declares war in trenchant manner. In a series of what in cinematic terms would be called 'jump-cuts', the scenes shift between Eastcheap where Nym, Pistol and Bardolph discuss in comic terms the poignant death of Sir John Falstaff, to the embarkation of the English army at Southampton, and to the French Court. Act Three finds Henry besieging Harfleur, urging on his troops to make the final effort – 'Once more unto the breach, dear friends' – to capture this important foothold in France. The French determine to avenge the loss of Harfleur by confronting the English King in Picardy, and in spite of their political disarray, confidently assemble a mighty army against the smaller English force at Agincourt. Act Four opens on the night before the battle, where in the English camp King Henry moves among his apprehensive troops. Equally apprehensive himself, Henry prays for fortitude for his men and pardon for his family 'O God of Battles...'. The day dawns in the French camp where the commanders anticipate the victory which lies before them. The English King, however, so stirs the hearts and minds of his soldiers in his 'Crispin Crispian' speech that his army achieves a famous victory. In defeat, the King of France, Charles VI, gives his daughter in matrimony to Henry, and agrees to acknowledge the English King as his heir.

Although the fervent patriotism of the play has displeased some critics, the period in which it was written should be borne in mind. It was a turbulent time for the English Crown, threatened by both Spain and France, with Catholic Ireland in revolt and Queen Elizabeth clearly reaching the end of her long life. As one of the Lord Chamberlain's Men, Shakespeare owed his living to the Court, so that his writing naturally supported the status quo. Laurence Olivier's 1944 film demonstrated the enduring effectiveness of the play's propaganda value half-a-century ago, though Michael Bogdanov's modern production for the English Shakespeare Company perhaps presents a more telling interpretation for the last decade of the twentieth century.

Details of Shakespeare's early life are scanty. He was the son of a prosperous merchant of Stratford-upon-Avon, and tradition has it that he was born on 23rd April 1564; records show that he was baptised three days later. It is likely that he attended the local grammar school, but he had no university education. Of his early career there is no record, though John Aubrey states that he was, for a time, a country schoolmaster. How he became involved with the stage is equally uncertain, but he was sufficiently established as a playwright by 1592 to be criticised in print. He was a leading member of the Lord Chamberlain's Company, which became the King's Men on the accession of James I in 1603. Shakespeare married Anne Hathaway in 1582, by whom he had two daughters and a son, Hamnet, who died in childhood. Towards the end of his life he loosened his ties with London, and retired to New Place, his substantial property in Stratford that he had bought in 1597. He died on 23rd April 1616 aged 52, and is buried in Holy Trinity Church, Stratford.

Further reading:

W A Armstrong: Shakespeare's Histories: An Anthology of Modern Criticism 1972
A Leggatt: Shakespeare's Political Drama. The History Plays and the Roman Plays 1978
R Ornstein: A Kingdom for a Stage: The Achievement of Shakespeare's History Plays 1972
M E Prior: The Drama of Power: Studies in Shakespeare's History Plays 1973
E Tillyard: Shakespeare's History Plays 1944, 1962

HENRY V

The Scene: first England, then France

CHARACTERS IN THE PLAY

Chorus

KING HENRY *the Fifth*

HUMPHREY, DUKE OF GLOUCESTER

JOHN OF LANCASTER, DUKE OF BEDFORD ⎱ *brothers to*

THOMAS OF LANCASTER, DUKE OF CLARENCE ⎰ *the king*

DUKE OF EXETER, *uncle to the king*

DUKE OF YORK, *cousin to the king, formerly Aumerle*

EARLS OF SALISBURY, WESTMORELAND, *and* WARWICK

ARCHBISHOP OF CANTERBURY

BISHOP OF ELY

EARL OF CAMBRIDGE

LORD SCROOP

SIR THOMAS GREY

SIR THOMAS ERPINGHAM, GOWER, FLUELLEN, MAC-MORRIS, JAMY, *officers in King Henry's army*

BATES, COURT, WILLIAMS, *soldiers in the same*

PISTOL, NYM, BARDOLPH

BOY. A *Herald*

CHARLES *the Sixth, King of France*

LEWIS, *the Dauphin*

DUKES *of* BURGUNDY, ORLEANS, BRITAINE *and* BOURBON

The Constable of France

RAMBURES, *and* GRANDPRÉ, *French Lords*

Governor of Harfleur

MONTJOY, *a French herald*

Ambassadors to the King of England

ISABEL, *Queen of France*

KATHARINE, *daughter to Charles and Isabel*

ALICE, *a lady attending upon her*

Hostess, formerly MRS QUICKLY, *now Pistol's wife*

Lords, Ladies, Officers, French and English Soldiers, Messengers, and Attendants

THE LIFE OF HENRY V

[I. Prologue]

Enter CHORUS

Chorus. O for a Muse of fire, that would ascend
The brightest heaven of invention:
A kingdom for a stage, princes to act,
And monarchs to behold the swelling scene.
Then should the warlike Harry, like himself,
Assume the port of Mars, and at his heels,
Leashed in like hounds, should Famine, Sword, and Fire
Crouch for employment. But pardon, gentles all,
The flat unraiséd spirits that hath dared
On this unworthy scaffold to bring forth   10
So great an object. Can this cockpit hold
The vasty fields of France? or may we cram
Within this wooden O the very casques
That did affright the air at Agincourt?
O, pardon! since a crooked figure may
Attest in little place a million;
And let us, ciphers to this great accompt,
On your imaginary forces work....
Suppose within the girdle of these walls
Are now confined two mighty monarchies,   20
Whose high upreared and abutting fronts
The perilous narrow ocean parts asunder.
Piece out our imperfections with your thoughts:
Into a thousand parts divide one man,
And make imaginary puissance.
Think, when we talk of horses, that you see them

Printing their proud hoofs i'th'receiving earth:
For 'tis your thoughts that now must deck our kings,
Carry them here and there: jumping o'er times;
30 Turning th'accomplishment of many years
Into an hour-glass: for the which supply,
Admit me Chorus to this history;
Who prologue-like your humble patience pray,
Gently to hear, kindly to judge, our play.   ['*exit.*'

[1. 1.]   London. *An antechamber in the King's palace*

Enter the ARCHBISHOP *of* CANTERBURY *and
the* BISHOP *of* ELY

Canterbury. My lord, I'll tell you—that self bill
        is urged,
Which in th' eleventh year of the last king's reign
Was like, and had indeed against us passed,
But that the scambling and unquiet time
Did push it out of farther question.
    Ely. But how, my lord, shall we resist it now?
    Canterbury. It must be thought on...If it pass
        against us,
We lose the better half of our possession:
For all the temporal lands which men devout
10 By testament have given to the Church
Would they strip from us; being valued thus—
As much as would maintain, to the king's honour,
Full fifteen earls, and fifteen hundred knights,
Six thousand and two hundred good esquires:
And, to relief of lazars and weak age,
Of indigent faint souls past corporal toil,
A hundred almshouses right well supplied:

And to the coffers of the king beside,
A thousand pounds by th'year: thus runs the bill.
 Ely. This would drink deep.
 Canterbury.   'Twould drink the cup and all. 20
 Ely. But what prevention?
 Canterbury. The king is full of grace and fair regard,
  and a true lover of the holy Church.
 Ely. The courses of his youth promised it not.
 Canterbury. The breath no sooner left his father's body,
But that his wildness, mortified in him,
Seemed to die too: yea, at that very moment,
Consideration like an angel came,
And whipped th' offending Adam out of him;
Leaving his body as a Paradise, 30
T'envelop and contain celestial spirits....
Never was such a sudden scholar made:
Never came reformation in a flood,
With such a heady currance, scouring faults:
Nor never Hydra-headed wilfulness
So soon did lose his seat—and all at once—
As in this king.
 Ely.   We are blessèd in the change.
 Canterbury. Hear him but reason in divinity;
And, all-admiring, with an inward wish
You would desire the king were made a prelate: 40
Hear him debate of commonwealth affairs;
You would say it hath been all in all his study:
List his discourse of war; and you shall hear
A fearful battle rendered you in music.
Turn him to any cause of policy,
The Gordian knot of it he will unloose,
Familiar as his garter: that, when he speaks,
The air, a chartered libertine, is still,
And the mute wonder lurketh in men's ears,

50 To steal his sweet and honeyed sentences:
So that the art and practic part of life
Must be the mistress to this theoric;
Which is a wonder, how his grace should glean it,
Since his addiction was to courses vain,
His companies unlettered, rude, and shallow,
His hours filled up with riots, banquets, sports;
And never noted in him any study,
Any retirement, any sequestration,
From open haunts and popularity.

60   *Ely*. The strawberry grows underneath the nettle,
And wholesome berries thrive and ripen best
Neighboured by fruit of baser quality:
And so the prince obscured his contemplation
Under the veil of wildness, which, no doubt,
Grew like the summer grass, fastest by night,
Unseen, yet crescive in his faculty.
   Canterbury. It must be so; for miracles are ceased:
And therefore we must needs admit the means
How things are perfected.
   Ely.   But, my good lord,

70 How now for mitigation of this bill
Urged by the commons? Doth his majesty
Incline to it, or no?
   Canterbury.   He seems indifferent—
Or rather swaying more upon our part
Than cherishing th' exhibiters against us:
For I have made an offer to his majesty,
Upon our spiritual convocation,
And in regard of causes now in hand,
Which I have opened to his grace at large,
As touching France, to give a greater sum

80 Than ever at one time the clergy yet
Did to his predecessors part withal.

Ely. How did this offer seem received, my lord?
Canterbury. With good acceptance of his majesty:
Save that there was not time enough to hear,
As I perceived his grace would fain have done,
The severals and unhidden passages
Of his true titles to some certain dukedoms,
And generally to the crown and seat of France
Derived from Edward, his great-grandfather.
Ely. What was th' impediment that broke this off?   90
Canterbury. The French ambassador upon that instant
Craved audience; and the hour, I think, is come
To give him hearing: is it four o'clock?
Ely. It is.
Canterbury. Then go we in, to know his embassy:
Which I could with a ready guess declare,
Before the Frenchman speak a word of it.
Ely. I'll wait upon you, and I long to hear it.
                                        [*they go*

[1. 2.]   *The Presence-chamber in the palace*
KING HENRY *in his chair of state;* GLOUCESTER,
BEDFORD, EXETER, WARWICK, WESTMORELAND *at a
table below; attendants*

King Henry. Where is my gracious Lord
    of Canterbury?
Exeter. Not here in presence.
King Henry.   Send for him, good uncle.
Westmoreland. Shall we call in th'ambassador,
    my liege?
King Henry. Not yet, my cousin: we would
    be resolved,
Before we hear him, of some things of weight
That task our thoughts, concerning us and France.

The Archbishop of CANTERBURY *and the Bishop of* ELY
enter and make obeisance

Canterbury. God and his angels guard your
 sacred throne,
And make you long become it!
 King Henry. Sure, we thank you....
My learnéd lord, we pray you to proceed,
10 And justly and religiously unfold
Why the law Salic that they have in France
Or should or should not bar us in our claim:
And God forbid, my dear and faithful lord,
That you should fashion, wrest, or bow your reading,
Or nicely charge your understanding soul
With opening titles miscreate, whose right
Suits not in native colours with the truth:
For God doth know how many now in health
Shall drop their blood in approbation
20 Of what your reverence shall incite us to.
Therefore take heed how you impawn our person,
How you awake our sleeping sword of war;
We charge you in the name of God, take heed:
For never two such kingdoms did contend
Without much fall of blood, whose guiltless drops
Are every one a woe, a sore complaint
'Gainst him whose wrongs gives edge unto the swords
That makes such waste in brief mortality....
Under this conjuration, speak, my lord:
30 For we will hear, note, and believe in heart,
That what you speak is in your conscience washed
As pure as sin with baptism.
 Canterbury. Then hear me, gracious sovereign, and
 you peers,
That owe yourselves, your lives, and services

To this imperial throne....There is no bar
To make against your highness' claim to France,
But this which they produce from Pharamond:
"In terram Salicam mulieres ne succedant"—
"No woman shall succeed in Salic land":
Which Salic land the French unjustly gloze   40
To be the realm of France, and Pharamond
The founder of this law and female bar.
Yet their own authors faithfully affirm
That the land Salic is in Germany,
Between the floods of Sala and of Elbe:
Where Charles the Great, having subdued the Saxons,
There left behind and settled certain French:
Who holding in disdain the German women
For some dishonest manners of their life,
Established then this law—to wit, no female   50
Should be inheritrix in Salic land:
Which Salic, as I said, 'twixt Elbe and Sala,
Is at this day in Germany called Meisen.
Then doth it well appear the Salic law
Was not deviséd for the realm of France:
Nor did the French possess the Salic land
Until four hundred one and twenty years
After defunction of King Pharamond,
Idly supposed the founder of this law,
Who died within the year of our redemption   60
Four hundred twenty-six: and Charles the Great
Subdued the Saxons, and did seat the French
Beyond the river Sala, in the year
Eight hundred five....Besides, their writers say,
King Pepin, which deposéd Childeric,
Did, as heir general, being descended
Of Blithild, which was daughter to King Clothair,
Make claim and title to the crown of France.

Hugh Capet also, who usurped the crown
70 Of Charles the duke of Lorraine, sole heir male
Of the true line and stock of Charles the Great,
To find his title with some shows of truth,
Though in pure truth it was corrupt and naught,
Conveyed himself as th'heir to th'Lady Lingare,
Daughter to Charlemain, who was the son
To Lewis the emperor, and Lewis the son
Of Charles the Great: also King Lewis the tenth,
Who was sole heir to the usurper Capet,
Could not keep quiet in his conscience,
80 Wearing the crown of France, till satisfied
That fair Queen Isabel, his grandmother,
Was lineal of the Lady Ermengare,
Daughter to Charles the foresaid duke of Lorraine:
By the which marriage the line of Charles the Great
Was re-united to the crown of France.
So that, as clear as is the summer's sun,
King Pepin's title and Hugh Capet's claim,
King Lewis his satisfaction, all appear
To hold in right and title of the female:
90 So do the kings of France unto this day.
Howbeit they would hold up this Salic law
To bar your highness claiming from the female,
And rather choose to hide them in a net
†Than amply to imbare their crooked titles,
Usurped from you and your progenitors.
    King Henry. May I with right and conscience make
        this claim?
    Canterbury. The sin upon my head, dread sovereign!
For in the book of Numbers is it writ,
When the man dies, let the inheritance
100 Descend unto the daughter....Gracious lord,
Stand for your own, unwind your bloody flag,

Look back into your mighty ancestors:
Go, my dread lord, to your great-grandsire's tomb,
From whom you claim; invoke his warlike spirit,
And your great-uncle's, Edward the Black Prince,
Who on the French ground played a tragedy,
Making defeat on the full power of France,
Whiles his most mighty father on a hill
Stood smiling to behold his lion's whelp
Forage in blood of French nobility....   110
O noble English, that could entertain
With half their forces the full pride of France,
And let another half stand laughing by,
All out of work and cold for action!

  Ely. Awake remembrance of these valiant dead,
And with your puissant arm renew their feats;
You are their heir, you sit upon their throne:
The blood and courage that renownéd them
Runs in your veins: and my thrice-puissant liege
Is in the very May-morn of his youth,   120
Ripe for exploits and mighty enterprises.

  Exeter. Your brother kings and monarchs of the earth
Do all expect that you should rouse yourself,
As did the former lions of your blood.

  Westmoreland. They know your grace hath cause, and
      means, and might;
So hath your highness: never king of England
Had nobles richer, and more loyal subjects,
Whose hearts have left their bodies here in England,
And lie pavilioned in the fields of France.

  Canterbury. O let their bodies follow, my dear liege, 130
With blood and sword and fire, to win your right:
In aid whereof, we of the spiritualty
Will raise your highness such a mighty sum
As never did the clergy at one time

Bring in to any of your ancestors.
 King Henry. We must not only arm t'invade
  the French,
But lay down our proportions to defend
Against the Scot, who will make road upon us
With all advantages.
140 *Canterbury*. They of those marches, gracious sovereign,
Shall be a wall sufficient to defend
Our inland from the pilfering borderers.
 King Henry. We do not mean the coursing
  snatchers only,
But fear the main intendment of the Scot,
Who hath been still a giddy neighbour to us:
For you shall read that my great-grandfather
Never went with his forces into France,
But that the Scot on his unfurnished kingdom
Came pouring like the tide into a breach,
150 With ample and brim fulness of his force,
Galling the gleanéd land with hot assays,
Girding with grievous siege castles and towns:
That England, being empty of defence,
Hath shook and trembled at th'ill neighbourhood.
 Canterbury. She hath been then more feared than
  harmed, my liege:
For hear her but exampled by herself—
When all her chivalry hath been in France,
And she a mourning widow of her nobles,
She hath herself not only well defended,
160 But taken and impounded as a stray
The King of Scots: whom she did send to France,
To fill King Edward's fame with prisoner kings,
And make her chronicle as rich with praise
As is the ooze and bottom of the sea
With sunken wrack and sumless treasuries.

Ely. But there's a saying very old and true—
　　"If that you will France win,
　　　Then with Scotland first begin:"
For once the eagle England being in prey,
To her unguarded nest the weasel Scot   170
Comes sneaking, and so sucks her princely eggs,
Playing the mouse in absence of the cat,
To 'tame and havoc more than she can eat.
　Exeter. It follows then the cat must stay at home.
Yet that is but a crushed necessity,
Since we have locks to safeguard necessaries,
And pretty traps to catch the petty thieves.
While that the arméd hand doth fight abroad
Th'adviséd head defends itself at home:
For government, though high, and low, and lower,   180
Put into parts, doth keep in one consent,
Congreeing in a full and natural close,
Like music.
　Canterbury.　　Therefore doth heaven divide
The state of man in divers functions,
Setting endeavour in continual motion:
To which is fixéd, as an aim or butt,
Obedience: for so work the honey-bees,
Creatures that by a rule in nature teach
The act of order to a peopled kingdom.
They have a king and officers of sorts: 190
Where some, like magistrates, correct at home,
Others, like merchants, venture trade abroad:
Others, like soldiers, arméd in their stings
Make boot upon the summer's velvet buds:
Which pillage they with merry march bring home
To the tent-royal of their emperor:
Who, busied in his majesty, surveys
The singing masons building roofs of gold,

2

The civil citizens kneading up the honey;
200 The poor mechanic porters crowding in
Their heavy burdens at his narrow gate:
The sad-eyed justice, with his surly hum,
Delivering o'er to executors pale
The lazy yawning drone...I this infer,
That many things, having full reference
To one consent, may work contrariously—
As many arrows loosèd several ways
Come to one mark:
†As many several ways meet in one town:
210 As many fresh streams meet in one salt sea:
As many lines close in the dial's centre:
So may a thousand actions, once afoot,
End in one purpose, and be all well borne
Without defeat....Therefore to France, my liege—
Divide your happy England into four,
Whereof take you one quarter into France,
And you withal shall make all Gallia shake.
If we, with thrice such powers left at home,
Cannot defend our own doors from the dog,
220 Let us be worried, and our nation lose
The name of hardiness and policy.
    King Henry. Call in the messengers sent from
        the Dauphin.   [*attendants go forth*
Now are we well resolved, and by God's help
And yours, the noble sinews of our power,
France being ours, we'll bend it to our awe,
Or break it all to pieces. Or there we'll sit,
Ruling in large and ample empery
O'er France and all her almost kingly dukedoms,
Or lay these bones in an unworthy urn,
230 Tombless, with no remembrance over them:
Either our history shall with full mouth

Speak freely of our acts, or else our grave,
Like Turkish mute, shall have a tongueless mouth,
Not worshipped with a waxen epitaph....

'*Enter* AMBASSADORS *of* FRANCE,' *followed by
a servitor, trundling a gilded barrel*

Now are we well prepared to know the pleasure
Of our fair cousin Dauphin: for we hear
Your greeting is from him, not from the king.
  Ambassador. May't please your majesty to give
      us leave
Freely to render what we have in charge:
Or shall we sparingly show you far off   240
The Dauphin's meaning and our embassy?
  King Henry. We are no tyrant, but a Christian king,
Unto whose grace our passion is as subject
As is our wretches fettered in our prisons;
Therefore with frank and with uncurbéd plainness
Tell us the Dauphin's mind.
  Ambassador.   Thus then, in few:
Your highness, lately sending into France,
Did claim some certain dukedoms, in the right
Of your great predecessor, King Edward the third.
In answer of which claim, the prince our master   250
Says that you savour too much of your youth,
And bids you be advised there's nought in France
That can be with a nimble galliard won:
You cannot revel into dukedoms there....
He therefore sends you, meeter for your spirit,
This tun of treasure; and, in lieu of this,
Desires you let the dukedoms that you claim
Hear no more of you....This the Dauphin speaks.
  King Henry. What treasure, uncle?
  Exeter. [*opening the barrel*] Tennis-balls, my liege.

260 *King Henry*. We are glad the Dauphin is so pleasant
        with us—
    His present and your pains we thank you for:
    When we have matched our rackets to these balls,
    We will in France, by God's grace, play a set
    Shall strike his father's crown into the hazard.
    Tell him he hath made a match with such a wrangler
    That all the courts of France will be disturbed
    With chases....And we understand him well,
    How he comes o'er us with our wilder days,
    Not measuring what use we made of them.
270 We never valued this poor seat of England,
    And therefore, living hence, did give ourself
    To barbarous licence: as 'tis ever common
    That men are merriest when they are from home....
    But tell the Dauphin I will keep my state,
    Be like a king, and show my sail of greatness,
    When I do rouse me in my throne of France.
    For that I have laid by my majesty,
    And plodded like a man for working-days:
    But I will rise there with so full a glory
280 That I will dazzle all the eyes of France,
    Yea, strike the Dauphin blind to look on us.
    And tell the pleasant prince this mock of his
    Hath turned his balls to gun-stones, and his soul
    Shall stand sore chargéd for the wasteful vengeance
    That shall fly with them: for many a thousand widows
    Shall this his mock mock out of their dear husbands;
    Mock mothers from their sons, mock castles down:
    And some are yet ungotten and unborn
    That shall have cause to curse the Dauphin's scorn.
290 But this lies all within the will of God,
    To whom I do appeal, and in whose name,
    Tell you the Dauphin, I am coming on,

To venge me as I may, and to put forth
My rightful hand in a well-hallowed cause.
So get you hence in peace...And tell the Dauphin
His jest will savour but of shallow wit,
When thousands weep more than did laugh at it....
Convey them with safe conduct. Fare you well.

['*Exeunt Ambassadors*'

Exeter. This was a merry message.

King Henry. We hope to make the sender blush at it: 300
Therefore, my lords, omit no happy hour
That may give furth'rance to our expedition:
For we have now no thought in us but France,
Save those to God, that run before our business.
Therefore let our proportions for these wars
Be soon collected, and all things thought upon
That may with reasonable swiftness add
More feathers to our wings: for, God before,
We'll chide this Dauphin at his father's door.
Therefore let every man now task his thought,   310
That this fair action may on foot be brought.

[*he rises and departs, the rest following*

[2. *Prologue*]

'*Flourish. Enter* CHORUS'

Chorus. Now all the youth of England are on fire,
And silken dalliance in the wardrobe lies:
Now thrive the armourers, and honour's thought
Reigns solely in the breast of every man.
They sell the pasture now, to buy the horse;
Following the mirror of all Christian kings,
With wingéd heels, as English Mercuries.
For now sits Expectation in the air,

And hides a sword, from hilts unto the point,
10 With crowns imperial, crowns and coronets,
Promised to Harry and his followers.
The French, advised by good intelligence
Of this most dreadful preparation,
Shake in their fear, and with pale policy
Seek to divert the English purposes.
O England! model to thy inward greatness,
Like little body with a mighty heart:
What might'st thou do, that honour would thee do,
Were all thy children kind and natural!
20 But see, thy fault France hath in thee found out,
A nest of hollow bosoms, which he fills
With treacherous crowns: and three corrupted men,
One, Richard Earl of Cambridge, and the second,
Henry Lord Scroop of Masham, and the third,
Sir Thomas Grey, knight of Northumberland,
Have for the gilt of France (O guilt indeed!)
Confirmed conspiracy with fearful France,
And by their hands this grace of kings must die,
If hell and treason hold their promises,
30 Ere he take ship for France, and in Southampton....
Linger your patience on, and we'll digest
Th'abuse of distance; force a play:
The sum is paid, the traitors are agreed,
The king is set from London, and the scene
Is now transported, gentles, to Southampton,
There is the playhouse now, there must you sit,
And thence to France shall we convey you safe,
And bring you back: charming the narrow seas
To give you gentle pass: for if we may,
40 We'll not offend one stomach with our play....
But till the king come forth, and not till then,
Unto Southampton do we shift our scene.   [*'exit'*]

[2. 1.]   *London. A street*

NYM and BARDOLPH meeting

Bardolph. Well met, Corporal Nym.

Nym. Good morrow, Lieutenant Bardolph.

Bardolph. What, are Ancient Pistol and you friends yet?

Nym. For my part, I care not: I say little: but when time shall serve, there shall be smiles—but that shall be as it may. I dare not fight, but I will wink and hold out mine iron: it is a simple one, but what though? It will toast cheese, and it will endure cold, as another man's sword will: and there's an end.   10

Bardolph. I will bestow a breakfast to make you friends, and we'll be all three sworn brothers to France: let't be so, good Corporal Nym.

Nym. Faith, I will live so long as I may, that's the certain of it: and when I cannot live any longer, I will do as I may: that is my rest, that is the rendezvous of it.

Bardolph. It is certain, corporal, that he is married to Nell Quickly, and certainly she did you wrong, for you were troth-plight to her.

Nym. I cannot tell—things must be as they may: men may sleep, and they may have their throats about them at that time, and some say knives have edges...It must be as it may—though patience be a tired mare, yet she will plod—there must be conclusions—well, I cannot tell.   20

Ancient PISTOL and the Hostess approach

Bardolph. Here comes Ancient Pistol and his wife: good corporal, be patient here.

†*Nym.* How now, mine host Pistol!

Pistol. Base tike, call'st thou me host?

30 Now by this hand I swear I scorn the term:
Nor shall my Nell keep lodgers.

Hostess. No, by my troth, not long: for we cannot
lodge and board a dozen or fourteen gentlewomen that
live honestly by the prick of their needles, but it will be
thought we keep a bawdy-house straight. [*Nym draws
his sword*] O well-a-day, Lady, if he be not hewn now,
we shall see wilful adultery and murder committed.

Bardolph.   Good lieutenant, good corporal, offer
nothing here.

40 *Nym*.   Pish!

Pistol.   Pish for thee, Iceland dog! thou prick-eared
cur of Iceland!

Hostess   Good Corporal Nym, show thy valour, and
put up your sword.

Nym.   Will you shog off? I would have you solus.

[*he sheathes his sword*

Pistol. 'Solus', egregious dog? O viper vile!
The 'solus' in thy most marvellous face,
The 'solus' in thy teeth, and in thy throat,
And in thy hateful lungs, yea in thy maw, perdy—
50 And, which is worse, within thy nasty mouth!
I do retort the 'solus' in thy bowels,
For I can take, and Pistol's cock is up,
And flashing fire will follow.

Nym.   I am not Barbason, you cannot conjure me:
I have an humour to knock you indifferently well...If
you grow foul with me, Pistol, I will scour you with my
rapier, as I may, in fair terms. If you would walk off,
I would prick your guts a little in good terms, as I may,
and that's the humour of it.

60 *Pistol*.   O braggart vile, and damnéd furious wight,
The grave doth gape, and doting death is near,
Therefore exhale!   [*they both draw*

Bardolph. [*also drawing*] Hear me, hear me what I
say: he that strikes the first stroke, I'll run him up to the
hilts, as I am a soldier.

Pistol. An oath of mickle might, and fury shall abate....
　　　　　　　　　　　　　　　　　　[*they sheathe*
Give me thy fist, thy fore-foot to me give:
Thy spirits are most tall.

Nym. I will cut thy throat one time or other in fair
terms, that is the humour of it.　　　　　　　　　　70

Pistol. 'Couple a gorge',
That is the word. I thee defy again.
O hound of Crete, think'st thou my spouse to get?
No, to the spital go,
And from the powdering-tub of infamy
Fetch forth the lazar kit of Cressid's kind,
Doll Tearsheet she by name, and her espouse.
I have, and I will hold, the quondam Quickly
For the only she: and—pauca, there's enough.
Go to.　　　　　　　　　　　　　　　　　80

'*Enter the* Boy'

Boy. Mine host Pistol, you must come to my master,
and you, hostess: he is very sick, and would to bed.
Good Bardolph, put thy face between his sheets, and do
the office of a warming-pan: faith, he's very ill.

Bardolph. Away, you rogue.　　　　[*the Boy runs off*
Hostess. By my troth, he'll yield the crow a pudding
one of these days...The king has killed his heart. Good
husband, come home presently.
　　　　　　　　　　　　　　　[*Hostess follows the Boy*
Bardolph. Come, shall I make you two friends? We
must to France together: why the devil should we keep　90
knives to cut one another's throats?

Pistol. Let floods o'erswell, and fiends for food howl on!

Nym. You'll pay me the eight shillings I won of you
at betting?

Pistol. Base is the slave that pays.

Nym. That now I will have: that's the humour of it.

Pistol. As manhood shall compound: push home.

[*they* 'draw'

Bardolph. By this sword, he that makes the first thrust,
I'll kill him: by this sword, I will.

100 *Pistol.* Sword is an oath, and oaths must have their
course.

Bardolph. Corporal Nym, an thou wilt be friends, be
friends, an thou wilt not, why then be enemies with
me too: prithee put up.

†*Nym.* I shall have my eight shillings I won of you
at betting?

Pistol. A noble shalt thou have, and present pay,
And liquor likewise will I give to thee,
And friendship shall combine, and brotherhood.

110 I'll live by Nym, and Nym shall live by me—
Is not this just? for I shall sutler be
Unto the camp, and profits will accrue.
Give me thy hand.   [*they sheathe again*

Nym. I shall have my noble?

Pistol. In cash, most justly paid.

Nym. Well, then that's the humour of 't.

[*they strike hands*

Hostess returns

Hostess. As ever you come of women, come in quickly
to Sir John. Ah, poor heart! he is so shaked of a burning
quotidian tertian, that it is most lamentable to behold.
120 Sweet men, come to him.

Nym. The king hath run bad humours on the knight,
that's the even of it.

Pistol. Nym, thou hast spoke the right,
His heart is fracted and corroborate.

Nym. The king is a good king, but it must be as it may:
he passes some humours and careers.

Pistol. Let us condole the knight, for, lambkins, we
will live.   [*they go*

[2. 2.]   *Southampton. A council-chamber*

'*Enter* EXETER, BEDFORD, *and* WESTMORELAND'

Bedford. 'Fore God, his grace is bold to trust
    these traitors.
Exeter. They shall be apprehended by and by.
Westmoreland. How smooth and even they do
    bear themselves,
As if allegiance in their bosoms sat
Crownéd with faith, and constant loyalty.
Bedford. The king hath note of all that they intend,
By interception which they dream not of.
Exeter. Nay, but the man that was his bedfellow,
Whom he hath dulled and cloyed with gracious favours—
That he should for a foreign purse so sell   10
His sovereign's life to death and treachery.

    Trumpets sound. '*Enter the King,* SCROOP,
    CAMBRIDGE, *and* GREY', *with attendants*

King Henry. Now sits the wind fair, and we
    will aboard....
My Lord of Cambridge, and my kind Lord of Masham,
And you, my gentle knight, give me your thoughts:
Think you not that the powers we bear with us
Will cut their passage through the force of France,

Doing the execution, and the act
For which we have in head assembled them?
  Scroop. No doubt, my liege, if each man do his best.
20 *King Henry.* I doubt not that, since we are
      well persuaded
We carry not a heart with us from hence,
That grows not in a fair consent with ours:
Nor leave not one behind, that doth not wish
Success and conquest to attend on us.
  Cambridge. Never was monarch better feared
      and loved
Than is your majesty; there's not, I think, a subject
That sits in heart-grief and uneasiness
Under the sweet shade of your government.
  Grey. True: those that were your father's enemies
30 Have steeped their galls in honey, and do serve you
With hearts create of duty and of zeal.
  King Henry. We therefore have great cause
      of thankfulness,
And shall forget the office of our hand
Sooner than quittance of desert and merit,
According to the weight and worthiness.
  Scroop. So service shall with steeléd sinews toil,
And labour shall refresh itself with hope
To do your grace incessant services.
  King Henry. We judge no less....Uncle of Exeter,
40 Enlarge the man committed yesterday,
That railed against our person: we consider
It was excess of wine that set him on,
And on his more advice we pardon him.
  Scroop. That's mercy, but too much security:
Let him be punished, sovereign, lest example
Breed, by his sufferance, more of such a kind.
  King Henry. O let us yet be merciful.

Cambridge. So may your highness, and yet punish too.
  Grey. Sir,
You show great mercy if you give him life,   50
After the taste of much correction.
  King Henry. Alas, your too much love and care of me
Are heavy orisons 'gainst this poor wretch...
If little faults, proceeding on distemper,
Shall not be winked at, how shall we stretch our eye
When capital crimes, chewed, swallowed, and digested,
Appear before us? We'll yet enlarge that man,
Though Cambridge, Scroop, and Grey, in their
        dear care
And tender preservation of our person
Would have him punished....And now to our   60
        French causes,   [*he takes up papers*
Who are the late commissioners?
  Cambridge. I one, my lord,
Your highness bade me ask for it to-day.
  Scroop. So did you me, my liege.
  Grey. And I, my royal sovereign.
  King Henry. [*delivering the papers*] Then, Richard,
        Earl of Cambridge, there is yours:
There yours, Lord Scroop of Masham: and, sir knight,
Grey of Northumberland, this same is yours:
Read them, and know I know your worthiness....
My Lord of Westmoreland, and uncle Exeter,   70
We will aboard to night....Why, how now, gentlemen?
What see you in those papers, that you lose
So much complexion? Look ye how they change:
Their cheeks are paper. Why, what read you there,
That have so cowarded and chased your blood
Out of appearance?   [*they fall upon their knee*
  Cambridge.   I do confess my fault,
And do submit me to your highness' mercy.

Grey. } To which we all appeal.
Scroop. }

King Henry. The mercy that was quick in us but late,
80 By your own counsel is suppressed and killed:
You must not dare, for shame, to talk of mercy,
For your own reasons turn into your bosoms,
As dogs upon their masters, worrying you...
See you, my princes, and my noble peers,
These English monsters: my Lord of Cambridge here,
You know how apt our love was to accord
To furnish him with all appertinents
Belonging to his honour; and this man
Hath for a few light crowns lightly conspired
90 And sworn unto the practices of France
To kill us here in Hampton. To the which
This knight, no less for bounty bound to us
Than Cambridge is, hath likewise sworn....But O,
What shall I say to thee, Lord Scroop, thou cruel,
Ingrateful, savage, and inhuman creature?
Thou that didst bear the key of all my counsels,
That knew'st the very bottom of my soul,
That (almost) mightst have coined me into gold,
Wouldst thou have practised on me, for thy use?
100 May it be possible, that foreign hire
Could out of thee extract one spark of evil
That might annoy my finger? 'Tis so strange,
That though the truth of it stands off as gross
†As black on white, my eye will scarcely see it.
Treason and murder ever kept together,
As two yoke-devils sworn to either's purpose,
Working so grossly in a natural cause,
That admiration did not hoop at them.
But thou, 'gainst all proportion, didst bring in
110 Wonder to wait on treason and on murder:

And whatsoever cunning fiend it was
That wrought upon thee so preposterously,
Hath got the voice in hell for excellence:
All other devils that suggest by treasons
Do botch and bungle up damnation,
With patches, colours, and with forms being fetched
From glist'ring semblances of piety:
But he that tempered thee, bade thee stand up,
Gave thee no instance why thou shouldst do treason,
Unless to dub thee with the name of traitor.   120
If that same demon that hath gulled thee thus
Should with his lion gait walk the whole world,
He might return to vasty Tartar back,
And tell the legions, "I can never win
A soul so easy as that Englishman's."
O, how hast thou with jealousy infected
The sweetness of affiance? Show men dutiful?
Why, so didst thou: seem they grave and learnéd?
Why, so didst thou: come they of noble family?
Why, so didst thou: seem they religious?   130
Why, so didst thou. Or are they spare in diet,
Free from gross passion, or of mirth, or anger,
Constant in spirit, not swerving with the blood,
Garnished and decked in modest complement,
Not working with the eye without the ear,
And but in purgéd judgement trusting neither?
Such and so finely bolted didst thou seem:
And thus thy fall hath left a kind of blot,
To mark the full-fraught man and best indued
With some suspicion. I will weep for thee.   140
For this revolt of thine, methinks, is like
Another fall of man....Their faults are open,
Arrest them to the answer of the law,
And God acquit them of their practices.

Exeter. I arrest thee of high treason, by the name of
Richard Earl of Cambridge.

I arrest thee of high treason, by the name of Henry
Lord Scroop of Masham.

I arrest thee of high treason, by the name of Thomas
150 Grey, knight of Northumberland.

Scroop. Our purposes God justly hath discovered,
And I repent my fault more than my death,
Which I beseech your highness to forgive,
Although my body pay the price of it.

Cambridge. For me, the gold of France did not seduce,
Although I did admit it as a motive,
The sooner to effect what I intended:
But God be thankéd for prevention,
Which I in sufferance heartily will rejoice,
160 Beseeching God, and you, to pardon me.

Grey. Never did faithful subject more rejoice
At the discovery of most dangerous treason,
Than I do at this hour joy o'er myself,
Prevented from a damnéd enterprise;
My fault, but not my body, pardon, sovereign.

King Henry. God quit you in his mercy! Hear
    your sentence.
You have conspired against our royal person,
Joined with an enemy proclaimed, and from his coffers
Received the golden earnest of our death:
170 Wherein you would have sold your king to slaughter,
His princes and his peers to servitude,
His subjects to oppression and contempt,
And his whole kingdom into desolation...
Touching our person, seek we no revenge,
But we our kingdom's safety must so tender,
Whose ruin you have sought, that to her laws
We do deliver you. Get you therefore hence,

Poor miserable wretches, to your death:
The taste whereof God of his mercy give
You patience to endure, and true repentance   180
Of all your dear offences....Bear them hence....
          [*Exeunt Cambridge, Scroop, and Grey, guarded*
Now, lords, for France: the enterprise whereof
Shall be to you as us, like glorious.
We doubt not of a fair and lucky war,
Since God so graciously hath brought to light
This dangerous treason lurking in our way
To hinder our beginnings. We doubt not now
But every rub is smoothéd on our way....
Then forth, dear countrymen: let us deliver
Our puissance into the hand of God,   190
Putting it traight in expedition....
Cheerly to sea, the signs of war advance,
No king of England, if not king of France.
          [*'Flourish'; they go*

[2. 3.]   *London. Before a tavern*

   Enter PISTOL, HOSTESS, NYM, BARDOLPH, *and* Boy

   Hostess. Prithee, honey-sweet husband, let me bring
thee to Staines.
   Pistol. No: for my manly heart doth earn.
Bardolph, be blithe: Nym, rouse thy vaunting veins:
Boy, bristle thy courage up: for Falstaff he is dead,
And we must earn therefore.
   Bardolph. Would I were with him, wheresome'er he
is, either in heaven or in hell!
   Hostess. Nay sure, he's not in hell: he's in Arthur's
bosom, if ever man went to Arthur's bosom: a' made 10
a finer end, and went away an it had been any christom

child: a' parted e'en just between twelve and one, e'en
at the turning o'th'tide: for after I saw him fumble with
the sheets, and play with flowers, and smile upon his
finger's end, I knew there was but one way: for his nose
was as sharp as a pen, and a' babbled of green fields.
'How now, Sir John?' quoth I. 'What, man! be o'
good cheer': so a' cried out, 'God, God, God!' three
or four times: now I, to comfort him, bid him a' should
20 not think of God; I hoped there was but one need to trouble
himself with any such thoughts yet: so a' bade me lay
more clothes on his feet: I put my hand into the bed,
and felt them, and they were as cold as any stone: then
I felt to his knees, and so up'ard and up'ard, and all was
as cold as any stone.

Nym. They say he cried out of sack.

Hostess. Ay, that a' did.

Bardolph. And of women.

Hostess. Nay, that a' did not.

30 *Boy.* Yes, that a' did, and said they were devils incarnate.

Hostess. A' could never abide carnation—'twas a colour
he never liked.

Boy. A' said once, the devil would have him about
women.

Hostess. A' did in some sort, indeed, handle women:
but then he was rheumatic, and talked of the whore of
Babylon.

Boy. Do you not remember a' saw a flea stick upon
Bardolph's nose, and a' said it was a black soul burning
40 in hell?

Bardolph. Well, the fuel is gone that maintained that
fire: that's all the riches I got in his service.

Nym. Shall we shog? the king will be gone from
Southampton.

Pistol. Come, let's away....My love, give me thy lips...

Look to my chattels and my movables:
Let senses rule: the word is 'Pitch and pay':
Trust none:
For oaths are straws, men's faiths are wafer-cakes,
And Hold-fast is the only dog, my duck: 50
Therefore, Caveto be thy counsellor....
Go, clear thy crystals....Yoke-fellows in arms,
Let us to France, like horse-leeches, my boys,
To suck, to suck, the very blood to suck!
  Boy. And that's but unwholesome food, they say.
  Pistol. Touch her soft mouth, and march.
  Bardolph. Farewell, hostess.   [*kissing her*
  Nym. I cannot kiss, that is the humour of it: but adieu.
  Pistol. Let housewifery appear: keep close, I thee
command.   60
  Hostess. Farewell: adieu.   [*they march off*

[2. 4.]   *The French King's Palace*

'*Flourish. Enter the French* KING, *the* DAUPHIN, *the
Dukes of* BERRI *and* BRITAINE,' *the* CONSTABLE, *and
others*

  French King. Thus comes the English with full power
      upon us,
And more than carefully it us concerns
To answer royally in our defences.
Therefore the Dukes of Berri and of Britaine,
Of Brabant and of Orleans, shall make forth,
And you, Prince Dauphin, with all swift dispatch
To line and new repair our towns of war
With men of courage and with means defendant:
For England his approaches makes as fierce
As waters to the sucking of a gulf.   10

It fits us then to be as provident
As fear may teach us, out of late examples
Left by the fatal and neglected English
Upon our fields.
    Dauphin.   My most redoubted father,
It is most meet we arm us 'gainst the foe:
For peace itself should not so dull a kingdom,
(Though war nor no known quarrel were in question)
But that defences, musters, preparations,
Should be maintained, assembled, and collected,
20 As were a war in expectation.
Therefore I say 'tis meet we all go forth
To view the sick and feeble parts of France:
And let us do it with no show of fear,
No, with no more than if we heard that England
Were busied with a Whitsun morris-dance:
For, my good liege, she is so idly kinged,
Her sceptre so fantastically borne
By a vain, giddy, shallow, humorous youth,
That fear attends her not.
    Constable.   O peace, Prince Dauphin!
30 You are too much mistaken in this king:
Question your grace the late ambassadors,
With what great state he heard their embassy,
How well supplied with noble counsellors,
How modest in exception; and, withal,
How terrible in constant resolution:
And you shall find his vanities forespent
Were but the outside of the Roman Brutus,
Covering discretion with a coat of folly;
As gardeners do with ordure hide those roots
40 That shall first spring, and be most delicate.
    Dauphin. Well, 'tis not so, my lord high constable.
But though we think it so, it is no matter:

In cases of defence, 'tis best to weigh
The enemy more mighty than he seems,
So the proportions of defence are filled:
Which, of a weak and niggardly projection,
Doth like a miser spoil his coat with scanting
A little cloth.

   French King. Think we King Harry strong:
And, princes, look you strongly arm to meet him.
The kindred of him hath been fleshed upon us: 50
And he is bred out of that bloody strain,
That haunted us in our familiar paths:
Witness our too much memorable shame,
When Cressy battle fatally was struck,
And all our princes captived, by the hand
Of that black name, Edward, Black Prince of Wales:
Whiles that his mountain sire, on mountain standing
Up in the air, crowned with the golden sun,
Saw his heroical seed, and smiled to see him
Mangle the work of nature, and deface   60
The patterns that by God and by French fathers
Had twenty years been made....This is a stem
Of that victorious stock: and let us fear
The native mightiness and fate of him.

            '*Enter a* MESSENGER'

   Messenger. Ambassadors from Harry King of England
Do crave admittance to your majesty.
   French King. We'll give them present audience. Go,
     and bring them.
               [*the Messenger departs, with certain lords*
You see this chase is hotly followed, friends.
   Dauphin. Turn head, and stop pursuit: for
     coward dogs

70 Most spend their mouths, when what they seem
        to threaten
   Runs far before them. Good my sovereign,
   Take up the English short, and let them know
   Of what a monarchy you are the head:
   Self-love, my liege, is not so vile a sin
   As self-neglecting.

   Re-enter LORDS, *with* EXETER *and his train*

   French King.   From our brother of England?
   Exeter. From him, and thus he greets your majesty:
   He wills you, in the name of God Almighty,
   That you divest yourself, and lay apart
   The borrowed glories that by gift of heaven,
80 By law of nature, and of nations, 'longs
   To him and to his heirs, namely, the crown,
   And all wide-stretchéd honours, that pertain
   By custom, and the ordinance of times,
   Unto the crown of France: that you may know
   'Tis no sinister, nor no awkward claim,
   Picked from the worm-holes of long-vanished days,
   Nor from the dust of old oblivion raked,
   He sends you this most memorable line, [*gives a paper*
   In every branch truly demonstrative;
90 Willing you overlook this pedigree:
   And when you find him evenly derived
   From his most famed of famous ancestors,
   Edward the third, he bids you then resign
   Your crown and kingdom, indirectly held
   From him the native and true challenger.
     French King. Or else what follows?
     Exeter. Bloody constraint: for if you hide the crown
   Even in your hearts, there will he rake for it.
   Therefore in fierce tempest is he coming,

In thunder and in earthquake, like a Jove: 100
That, if requiring fail, he will compel.
And bids you, in the bowels of the Lord,
Deliver up the crown, and to take mercy
On the poor souls, for whom this hungry war
Opens his vasty jaws: and on your head
Turning the widows' tears, the orphans' cries,
The dead men's blood, the pining maidens' groans,
For husbands, fathers, and betrothéd lovers,
That shall be swallowed in this controversy.
This is his claim, his threatening, and my message: 110
Unless the Dauphin be in presence here;
To whom expressly I bring greeting too.
 French King. For us, we will consider of this further:
To-morrow shall you bear our full intent
Back to our brother of England.
 Dauphin.   For the Dauphin,
I stand here for him: what to him from England?
 Exeter. Scorn and defiance, slight regard, contempt,
And any thing that may not misbecome
The mighty sender, doth he prize you at.
Thus says my king: an if your father's highness   120
Do not, in grant of all demands at large,
Sweeten the bitter mock you sent his majesty,
He'll call you to so hot an answer of it,
That caves and womby vaultages of France
Shall chide your trespass, and return your mock
In second accent of his ordinance.
 Dauphin. Say: if my father render fair return,
It is against my will; for I desire
Nothing but odds with England. To that end,
As matching to his youth and vanity,   130
I did present him with the Paris-balls.
 Exeter. He'll make your Paris Louvre shake for it,

Were it the mistress-court of mighty Europe:
And, be assured, you'll find a difference,
As we his subjects have in wonder found,
Between the promise of his greener days,
And these he masters now: now he weighs time
Even to the utmost grain: that you shall read
In your own losses, if he stay in France.

140 *French King* [*rises*] To-morrow shall you know our
            mind at full.   ['*Flourish*'

  Exeter. Dispatch us with all speed, lest that our king
Come here himself to question our delay;
For he is footed in this land already.

  French King. You shall be soon dispatched, with
            fair conditions.
A night is but small breath, and little pause,
To answer matters of this consequence.
                    [*the King and his Courtiers leave,*
                        Exeter with his train following

[3. Prologue]

'*Flourish. Enter* CHORUS'

  Chorus. Thus with imagined wing our swift scene flies,
In motion of no less celerity
Than that of thought....Suppose that you have seen
The well-appointed king at Hampton pier
Embark his royalty: and his brave fleet
With silken streamers the young Phœbus fanning;
Play with your fancies: and in them behold,
Upon the hempen tackle, ship-boys climbing;
Hear the shrill whistle, which doth order give
10 To sounds confused: behold the threaden sails,
Borne with th'invisible and creeping wind,

Draw the huge bottoms through the furrowed sea,
Breasting the lofty surge....O, do but think
You stand upon the rivage, and behold
A city on th'inconstant billows dancing:
For so appears this fleet majestical,
Holding due course to Harfleur....Follow, follow!
Grapple your minds to sternage of this navy,
And leave your England as dead midnight, still,
Guarded with grandsires, babies, and old women,   20
Either past or not arrived to pith and puissance...
For who is he, whose chin is but enriched
With one appearing hair, that will not follow
These culled and choice-drawn cavaliers to France?
Work, work your thoughts, and therein see a siege:
Behold the ordinance on their carriages,
With fatal mouths gaping on girded Harfleur....
Suppose th'ambassador from the French comes back:
Tells Harry that the king doth offer him
Katharine his daughter, and with her, to dowry,   30
Some petty and unprofitable dukedoms.
The offer likes not: and the nimble gunner
With linstock now the devilish cannon touches,
          ['*Alarum, and chambers go off*'
And down goes all before them....Still be kind,
And eke out our performance with your mind.
                   ['*exit*'

[3. 1.]   *France. Before the gates* '*at Harfleur*'

'*Alarum.*' '*Enter the King*, EXETER, BEDFORD, *and*
GLOUCESTER,' *followed by soldiers with* '*scaling ladders*'

   King Henry.   Once more unto the breach, dear friends,
      once more;
Or close the wall up with our English dead...

In peace, there's nothing so becomes a man,
As modest stillness, and humility:
But when the blast of war blows in our ears,
Then imitate the action of the tiger:
†Stiffen the sinews, conjure up the blood,
Disguise fair nature with hard-favoured rage:
Then lend the eye a terrible aspect:
10 Let it pry through the portage of the head,
Like the brass cannon: let the brow o'erwhelm it
As fearfully as doth a galléd rock
O'erhang and jutty his confounded base,
Swilled with the wild and wasteful ocean.
Now set the teeth, and stretch the nostril wide,
Hold hard the breath, and bend up every spirit
To his full height! On, on, you noblest English,
Whose blood is fet from fathers of war-proof:
Fathers, that like so many Alexanders,
20 Have in these parts from morn till even fought,
And sheathed their swords for lack of argument.
Dishonour not your mothers: now attest
That those whom you called fathers did beget you!
Be copy now to men of grosser blood,
And teach them how to war! And you, good yeomen,
Whose limbs were made in England; show us here
The mettle of your pasture: let us swear,
That you are worth your breeding—which I doubt not:
For there is none of you so mean and base,
30 That hath not noble lustre in your eyes.
I see you stand like greyhounds in the slips,
Straining upon the start. The game's afoot:
Follow your spirit; and upon this charge,
Cry, 'God for Harry, England, and Saint George!'

                         [*They pass forward to the breach.*
                              '*Alarum, and chambers go off*'

[3. 2.] 'NYM, BARDOLPH, PISTOL,' and the
        'Boy' come up

Bardolph. On, on, on, on, on! to the breach, to the
breach!

Nym. Pray thee, corporal, stay, the knocks are too hot:
and for mine own part, I have not a case of lives: the
humour of it is too hot, that is the very plain-song of it.

Pistol. The plain-song is most just: for humours
    do abound:
Knocks go and come: God's vassals drop and die:
        And sword and shield,
        In bloody field,
        Doth win immortal fame.   10

Boy. Would I were in an alehouse in London! I would
give all my fame for a pot of ale, and safety.

Pistol. And I:
        If wishes would prevail with me,
        My purpose should not fail with me;
            But thither would I hie.

Boy. As duly,
        But not as truly,
            As bird doth sing on bough.

*FLUELLEN marches up with supply troops for the breach;
he belabours Bardolph, Nym and Pistol with the flat of
his sword; the Boy hides behind a bush*

Fluellen. Up to the breach, you dogs; avaunt, you 20
cullions!

Pistol. Be merciful, great duke, to men of mould:
Abate thy rate, abate thy manly rage;
Abate thy rage, great duke!
Good bawcock, bate thy rage: use lenity, sweet chuck!

Nym. These be good humours...Your honour wins bad
humours.   [*Fluellen drives them forward with his men*

Boy. [*stealing forth*] As young as I am, I have observed
these three swashers: I am boy to them all three, but all
30 they three, though they would serve me, could not be
man to me; for indeed three such antics do not amount
to a man...For Bardolph, he is white-livered and red-
faced; by the means whereof a' faces it out, but fights
not: for Pistol, he hath a killing tongue, and a quiet
sword; by the means whereof a' breaks words, and keeps
whole weapons: for Nym, he hath heard that men of
few words are the best men, and therefore he scorns to
say his prayers, lest a' should be thought a coward: but
his few bad words are matched with as few good deeds;
40 for a' never broke any man's head but his own, and that
was against a post, when he was drunk. They will steal
any thing, and call it purchase. Bardolph stole a lute-
case, bore it twelve leagues, and sold it for three half-
pence. Nym and Bardolph are sworn brothers in
filching: and in Calais they stole a fire-shovel. I knew
by that piece of service, the men would carry coals. They
would have me as familiar with men's pockets as their
gloves or their handkerchers: which makes much against
my manhood, if I should take from another's pocket, to
50 put into mine; for it is plain pocketing up of wrongs....
I must leave them, and seek some better service: their
villany goes against my weak stomach, and therefore I
must cast it up.   [*he goes back towards the camp*

FLUELLEN *returns with* GOWER

Gower. Captain Fluellen, you must come presently to
the mines; the Duke of Gloucester would speak with you.
Fluellen. To the mines? Tell you the duke, it is not
so good to come to the mines: for look you, the mines
is not according to the disciplines of the war; the con-
cavities of it is not sufficient: for look you, th'athversary—

you may discuss unto the duke—look you, is digt himself 60
four yard under the counter-mines: by Cheshu, I think
a' will plow up all, if there is not better directions.

Gower. The Duke of Gloucester, to whom the order
of the siege is given, is altogether directed by an Irish-
man, a very valiant gentleman, i'faith.

Fluellen. It is Captain Macmorris, is it not?

Gower. I think it be.

Fluellen. By Cheshu, he is an ass, as in the world,
I will verify as much in his beard: he has no more
directions in the true disciplines of the wars, look you, 70
of the Roman disciplines, than is a puppy-dog.

'*Enter MACMORRIS and Captain JAMY*'

Gower. Here a' comes, and the Scots captain, Captain
Jamy, with him.

Fluellen. Captain Jamy is a marvellous falorous gentleman, that is certain, and of great expedition and
knowledge in th'ancient wars, upon my particular
knowledge of his directions: by Cheshu, he will maintain his argument as well as any military man in the
world, in the disciplines of the pristine wars of the
Romans.   80

Jamy. I say gud-day, Captain Fluellen.

Fluellen. God-den to your worship, good Captain
James.

Gower. How now, Captain Macmorris, have you quit
the mines? have the pioners given o'er?

Macmorris. By Chrish, la! tish ill done: the work ish
give over, the trompet sound the retreat. By my hand
I swear, and my father's soul, the work ish ill done:
it ish give over: I would have blowed up the town, so
Chrish save me, la, in an hour. O tish ill done, tish ill 90
done: by my hand, tish ill done!

Fluellen. Captain Macmorris, I beseech you now, will you voutsafe me, look you, a few disputations with you, as partly touching or concerning the disciplines of the war, the Roman wars, in the way of argument, look you, and friendly communication: partly to satisfy my opinion, and partly for the satisfaction, look you, of my mind: as touching the direction of the military discipline, that is the point.

100 *Jamy.* It sall be vary gud, gud feith, gud captains bath, and I sall quit you with gud leve, as I may pick occasion: that sall I, marry.

Macmorris. It is no time to discourse, so Chrish save me: the day is hot, and the weather, and the wars, and the king, and the dukes: it is no time to discourse, the town is beseeched: an the trumpet call us to the breach, and we talk, and, be Chrish, do nothing, 'tis shame for us all: so God sa' me, 'tis shame to stand still, it is shame, by my hand: an there is throats to be cut, and works to 110 be done, and there ish nothing done, so Chrish sa' me, la!

Jamy. By the mess, ere these eyes of mine take themselves to slomber, ay'll de gude service, or ay'll lig i'th'grund for it; ay, or go to death: and ay'll pay't as valorously as I may, that sal I suerly do, that is the breff and the long...Mary, I wad full fain hear some question 'tween you tway.

Fluellen. Captain Macmorris, I think, look you, under your correction, there is not many of your nation—

Macmorris. Of my nation! What ish my nation? Ish 120 a villain, and a bastard, and a knave, and a rascal— What ish my nation? Who talks of my nation?

Fluellen. Look you, if you take the matter otherwise than is meant, Captain Macmorris, peradventure I shall think you do not use me with that affability as in discretion you ought to use me, look you, being as good

a man as yourself, both in the disciplines of war, and in
the derivation of my birth, and in other particularities.

Macmorris. I do not know you so good a man as
myself: so Chrish save me, I will cut off your head.

Gower. Gentlemen both, you will mistake each other. 130
Jamy. Ah! that's a foul fault.

'*A parley*' *sounded from the walls*

Gower. The town sounds a parley.
Fluellen. Captain Macmorris, when there is more
better opportunity to be required, look you, I will be
so bold as to tell you I know the disciplines of war: and
there is an end.   [*they stand aside*

[3. 3.] *The* GOVERNOR *and some* CITIZENS *appear upon
the walls.* '*Enter the King and all his train before
the gates*'

King. How yet resolves the governor of the town?
This is the latest parle we will admit:
Therefore to our best mercy give yourselves,
Or, like to men proud of destruction,
Defy us to our worst: for, as I am a soldier,
A name that in my thoughts becomes me best,
If I begin the battery once again,
I will not leave the half-achieved Harfleur
Till in her ashes she lie buriéd.
The gates of mercy shall be all shut up,   10
And the fleshed soldier, rough and hard of heart,
In liberty of bloody hand, shall range
With conscience wide as hell, mowing like grass
Your fresh fair virgins, and your flowering infants.
What is it then to me, if impious war,
Arrayed in flames like to the prince of fiends,
Do with his smirched complexion all fell feats

Enlinked to waste and desolation?
What is't to me, when you yourselves are cause,
20 If your pure maidens fall into the hand
Of hot and forcing violation?
What rein can hold licentious wickedness,
When down the hill he holds his fierce career?
We may as bootless spend our vain command
Upon th'enragéd soldiers in their spoil,
As send precépts to the leviathan
To come ashore. Therefore, you men of Harfleur,
Take pity of your town and of your people,
Whiles yet my soldiers are in my command,
30 Whiles yet the cool and temperate wind of grace
O'erblows the filthy and contagious clouds
Of heady murder, spoil, and villany.
If not—why, in a moment look to see
The blind and bloody soldier with foul hand
Defile the locks of your shrill-shrieking daughters:
Your fathers taken by the silver beards,
And their most reverend heads dashed to the walls:
Your naked infants spitted upon pikes,
Whiles the mad mothers with their howls confused
40 Do break the clouds; as did the wives of Jewry,
At Herod's bloody-hunting slaughtermen.
What say you? Will you yield, and this avoid?
Or, guilty in defence, be thus destroyed?
   Governor. Our expectation hath this day an end:
The Dauphin, whom of succours we entreated,
Returns us that his powers are yet not ready
To raise so great a siege...Therefore, great king,
We yield our town and lives to thy soft mercy:
Enter our gates, dispose of us and ours,
50 For we no longer are defensible.
   King. Open your gates...Come, uncle Exeter,

Go you and enter Harfleur; there remain,
And fortify it strongly 'gainst the French:
Use mercy to them all. For us, dear uncle,
The winter coming on, and sickness growing
Upon our soldiers, we will retire to Calais.
To-night in Harfleur will we be your guest,
To-morrow for the march are we addrest.

['*Flourish.*' *The King and his forces 'enter the town*'

[3. 4.]   *Rouen. The French King's palace*

The Princess KATHARINE *and* ALICE, '*an old
Gentlewoman*', *and other ladies-in-waiting*

Katharine. Alice, tu as été en Angleterre, et tu bien
parles le langage.

Alice. Un peu, madame.

Katharine. Je te prie, m'enseignez—il faut que j'ap-
prenne à parler...Comment appelez-vous la main en
Anglais?

Alice. La main? elle est appelée de hand.

Katharine. De hand. Et les doigts?

Alice. Les doigts? ma foi, j'oublie les doigts; mais je
me souviendrai. Les doigts? je pense qu'ils sont appelés 10
de fingres: oui, de fingres.

Katharine. La main, de hand: les doigts, de fingres.
Je pense que je suis le bon écolier. J'ai gagné deux mots
d'Anglais vitement. Comment appelez-vous les ongles?

Alice. Les ongles? nous les appelons de nailès.

Katharine. De nailès. Écoutez: dites moi si je parle
bien: de hand, de fingres, et de nailès.

Alice. C'est bien dit, madame; il est fort bon Anglais.

Katharine. Dites moi l'Anglais pour le bras.

Alice. De arm, madame.   20

4   PSHV

Katharine. Et le coude.

Alice. D' elbow.

Katharine. D' elbow. Je m'en fais la répétition de tous les mots que vous m'avez appris dès à présent.

Alice. Il est trop difficile, madame, comme je pense.

Katharine. Excusez-moi, Alice; écoutez: d' hand, de fingre, de nailès, d' arma, de bilbow.

Alice. D' elbow, madame.

Katharine. O Seigneur Dieu, je m'en oublie! d' elbow. Comment appelez-vous le col?

Alice. De nick, madame.

Katharine. De nick. Et le menton?

Alice. De chin.

Katharine. De sin. Le col, de nick: le menton, de sin.

Alice. Oui. Sauf votre honneur, en vérité, vous prononcez les mots aussi droit que les natifs d'Angleterre.

Katharine. Je ne doute point d'apprendre, par la grace de Dieu, et en peu de temps.

Alice. N'avez vous pas déjà oublié ce que je vous ai enseigné?

Katharine. Non, je réciterai à vous promptement: d' hand, de fingre, de mailès,—

Alice. De nailès, madame.

Katharine. De nailès, de arm, de ilbow.

Alice. Sauf votre honneur, d' elbow.

Katharine. Ainsi dis-je: d' elbow, de nick, et de sin. Comment appelez-vous le pied et la robe?

Alice. Le foot, madame, et le count.

Katharine. Le foot, et le count? O Seignieur Dieu! ils sont mots de son mauvais, corruptible, gros, et impudique, et non pour les dames d'honneur d'user: je ne voudrais prononcer ces mots devant les seigneurs de France pour tout le monde. Foh! le foot et le count. Néanmoins, je réciterai une autre fois ma leçon ensemble:

d' hand, de fingre, de nailès, d' arm, d' elbow, de nick,
de sin, de foot, le count.

Alice. Excellent, madame!

Katharine. C'est assez pour une fois: allons-nous à
dîner.   [*they go*

[3. 5.] '*Enter the* KING *of France, the* DAUPHIN,' *the
Duke of* BRITAINE, '*the* CONSTABLE *of France, and
others*'

French King. 'Tis certain he hath passed the
        river Somme.

Constable. And if he be not fought withal, my lord,
Let us not live in France: let us quit all,
And give our vineyards to a barbarous people.

Dauphin. O Dieu vivant! shall a few sprays of us,
The emptying of our fathers' luxury,
Our scions, put in wild and savage stock,
Spirt up so suddenly into the clouds,
And overlook their grafters?

Britaine. Normans, but bastard Normans,
        Norman bastards!   10
Mort Dieu! ma vie! if they march along
Unfought withal, but I will sell my dukedom,
To buy a slobbery and a dirty farm
In that nook-shotten isle of Albion.

Constable. Dieu de batailles! where have they
        this mettle?
Is not their climate foggy, raw, and dull?
On whom, as in despite, the sun looks pale,
Killing their fruit with frowns. Can sodden water,
A drench for sur-reined jades, their barley broth,
Decoct their cold blood to such valiant heat?   20
And shall our quick blood, spirited with wine,
Seem frosty? O, for honour of our land,

Let us not hang like roping icicles
Upon our houses' thatch, whiles a more frosty people
Sweat drops of gallant youth in our rich fields...
Poor we may call them in their native lords.
  Dauphin. By faith and honour,
Our madams mock at us, and plainly say
Our mettle is bred out, and they will give
30 Their bodies to the lust of English youth,
To new-store France with bastard warriors.
  Britaine. They bid us to the English dancing-
    schools,
And teach lavoltas high, and swift corantos,
Saying our grace is only in our heels,
And that we are most lofty runaways.
  French King. Where is Montjoy the herald? speed
    him hence,
Let him greet England with our sharp defiance....
Up, princes, and, with spirit of honour edged
More sharper than your swords, hie to the field:
40 Charles Delabreth, high constable of France,
You Dukes of Orleans, Bourbon, and of Berri,
Alençon, Brabant, Bar, and Burgundy,
Jacques Chatillon, Rambures, Vaudemont,
Beaumont, Grandpré, Roussi, and Faulconbridge,
Foix, Lestrake, Bouciqualt, and Charolois,
High dukes, great princes, barons, lords, and knights;
For your great seats now quit you of great shames...
Bar Harry England, that sweeps through our land
With pennons painted in the blood of Harfleur:
50 Rush on his host, as doth the melted snow
Upon the valleys, whose low vassal seat
The Alps doth spit and void his rheum upon....
Go down upon him—you have power enough—
†And in a chariot, captive into Rouen

Bring him our prisoner.

Constable.   This becomes the great.
Sorry am I his numbers are so few,
His soldiers sick and famished in their march:
For I am sure, when he shall see our army,
He'll drop his heart into the sink of fear,
And for achievement offer us his ransom.   60

French King. Therefore, lord constable, haste
     on Montjoy,
And let him say to England, that we send
To know what willing ransom he will give....
Prince Dauphin, you shall stay with us in Rouen.

Dauphin. Not so, I do beseech your majesty.

French King. Be patient, for you shall remain
     with us....
Now forth, lord constable and princes all,
And quickly bring us word of England's fall. [*they go*

[3. 6.]   *Near a river in Picardy*

The English and Welsh captains, GOWER and
FLUELLEN, meeting

Gower. How now, Captain Fluellen! come you from
the bridge?

Fluellen. I assure you, there is very excellent services
committed at the bridge.

Gower. Is the Duke of Exeter safe?

Fluellen. The Duke of Exeter is as magnanimous as
Agamemnon, and a man that I love and honour with
my soul, and my heart, and my duty, and my live, and
my living, and my uttermost power. He is not—God be
praised and blessed!—any hurt in the world, but keeps 10
the bridge most valiantly, with excellent discipline.

There is an ancient lieutenant there at the pridge, I think in my very conscience he is as valiant a man as Mark Antony, and he is a man of no estimation in the world, but I did see him do as gallant service.

Gower. What do you call him?

Fluellen. He is called Ancient Pistol.

Gower. I know him not.

PISTOL *is seen approaching*

Fluellen. Here is the man.

20 *Pistol.* Captain, I thee beseech to do me favours: The Duke of Exeter doth love thee well.

Fluellen. Ay, I praise God, and I have merited some love at his hands.

Pistol. Bardolph, a soldier firm and sound of heart, And of buxom valour, hath, by cruel fate, And giddy Fortune's furious fickle wheel, That goddess blind, That stands upon the rolling restless stone—

Fluellen. By your patience, Ancient Pistol...Fortune 30 is painted blind, with a muffler afore his eyes, to signify to you that Fortune is blind; and she is painted also with a wheel, to signify to you, which is the moral of it, that she is turning and inconstant, and mutability, and variation: and her foot, look you, is fixed upon a spherical stone, which rolls, and rolls, and rolls: in good truth, the poet makes a most excellent description of it: Fortune is an excellent moral.

Pistol. Fortune is Bardolph's foe, and frowns on him: For he hath stolen a pax, and hangéd must a' be 40 A damnéd death!

Let gallows gape for dog, let man go free, And let not hemp his wind-pipe suffocate: But Exeter hath given the doom of death,

For pax of little price.
Therefore go speak, the duke will hear thy voice;
And let not Bardolph's vital thread be cut
With edge of penny cord, and vile reproach.
Speak, captain, for his life, and I will thee requite.
Fluellen. Ancient Pistol, I do partly understand
    your meaning.
Pistol. Why then rejoice therefore.   50
Fluellen. Certainly, ancient, it is not a thing to
rejoice at: for if, look you, he were my brother, I would
desire the duke to use his good pleasure, and put him
to execution; for discipline ought to be used.
Pistol. Die and be damned! and figo for thy friendship!
                        [he turns away
Fluellen. It is well.
Pistol. [*he bites his thumb*] The fig of Spain!
Fluellen. Very good.
Gower. Why, this is an arrant counterfeit rascal, I
remember him now: a bawd, a cutpurse.   60
Fluellen. I'll assure you, a' uttered as prave words at
the pridge as you shall see in a summer's day: but it is
very well: what he has spoke to me, that is well, I warrant
you, when time is serve.
Gower. Why, 'tis a gull, a fool, a rogue, that now and
then goes to the wars, to grace himself at his return into
London, under the form of a soldier...And such fellows
are perfect in the great commanders' names, and they
will learn you by rote where services were done; at such
and such a sconce, at such a breach, at such a convoy: 70
who came off bravely, who was shot, who disgraced,
what terms the enemy stood on; and this they con
perfectly in the phrase of war, which they trick up with
new-tuned oaths: and what a beard of the general's cut,
and a horrid suit of the camp, will do among foaming

bottles, and ale-washed wits, is wonderful to be thought
on. But you must learn to know such slanders of the age,
or else you may be marvellously mistook.

Fluellen. I tell you what, Captain Gower: I do per-
80 ceive he is not the man that he would gladly make show
to the world he is: if I find a hole in his coat, I will tell
him my mind...[*Drum heard*] Hark you, the king is
coming, and I must speak with him from the pridge.

'*Drum and colours. Enter King*' HENRY, GLOUCESTER,
'*and his poor soldiers*'

Fluellen. God pless your majesty!

King Henry. How now, Fluellen, cam'st thou from
the bridge?

Fluellen. Ay, so please your majesty...The Duke of
Exeter has very gallantly maintained the pridge; the
French is gone off, look you, and there is gallant and
90 most prave passages: marry, th'athversary was have
possession of the pridge, but he is enforced to retire, and
the Duke of Exeter is master of the pridge...I can tell
your majesty, the duke is a prave man.

King Henry. What men have you lost, Fluellen?

Fluellen. The perdition of th'athversary hath been
very great, reasonable great: marry, for my part, I think
the duke hath lost never a man, but one that is like to be
executed for robbing a church, one Bardolph, if your
majesty know the man: his face is all bubukles and
100 whelks, and knobs, and flames afire, and his lips blows
at his nose, and it is like a coal of fire, sometimes plue,
and sometimes red, but his nose is executed, and his
fire's out.

King Henry. We would have all such offenders so cut
off: and we give express charge that in our marches
through the country there be nothing compelled from

the villages; nothing taken but paid for; none of the
French upbraided or abused in disdainful language;
for when lenity and cruelty play for a kingdom, the
gentler gamester is the soonest winner.   110

A 'tucket' sounds. MONTJOY *approaches*

Montjoy. You know me by my habit.

King Henry. Well then, I know thee: what shall I
know of thee?

Montjoy. My master's mind.

King Henry. Unfold it.

Montjoy. Thus says my king: Say thou to Harry of
England, Though we seemed dead, we did but sleep:
advantage is a better soldier than rashness....Tell him,
we could have rebuked him at Harfleur, but that we
thought not good to bruise an injury till it were full 120
ripe. Now we speak upon our cue, and our voice is
imperial: England shall repent his folly, see his weak-
ness, and admire our sufferance. Bid him therefore
consider of his ransom, which must proportion the losses
we have borne, the subjects we have lost, the disgrace
we have digested; which in weight to re-answer, his
pettiness would bow under. For our losses, his exchequer
is too poor; for th'effusion of our blood, the muster of
his kingdom too faint a number; and for our disgrace,
his own person kneeling at our feet, but a weak and 130
worthless satisfaction....To this add defiance: and tell
him, for conclusion, he hath betrayed his followers,
whose condemnation is pronounced...So far my king
and master; so much my office.

King Henry. What is thy name? I know thy quality.

Montjoy. Montjoy.

King Henry. Thou dost thy office fairly. Turn
     thee back,

And tell thy king I do not seek him now,
But could be willing to march on to Calais
140 Without impeachment: for, to say the sooth,
Though 'tis no wisdom to confess so much
Unto an enemy of craft and vantage,
My people are with sickness much enfeebled,
My numbers lessened: and those few I have,
Almost no better than so many French;
Who when they were in health, I tell thee, herald,
I thought upon one pair of English legs
Did march three Frenchmen....Yet forgive me, God,
That I do brag thus! This your air of France
150 Hath blown that vice in me. I must repent...
Go therefore, tell thy master here I am;
My ransom is this frail and worthless trunk;
My army, but a weak and sickly guard:
Yet, God before, tell him we will come on,
Though France himself, and such another neighbour,
Stand in our way....There's for thy labour, Montjoy.
                              [*he gives a purse of gold*
Go bid thy master well advise himself.
If we may pass, we will: if we be hindered,
We shall your tawny ground with your red blood
160 Discolour...And so, Montjoy, fare you well.
The sum of all our answer is but this:
We would not seek a battle as we are,
Nor, as we are, we say we will not shun it:
So tell your master.
     Montjoy. I shall deliver so...Thanks to your highness.
                              [*he bows low and departs*
     Gloucester. I hope they will not come upon us now.
     King Henry. We are in God's hand, brother, not
          in theirs...
March to the bridge—it now draws toward night—

Beyond the river we'll encamp ourselves,
And on to-morrow bid them march away.   [*they go* 170

[3. 7.]   *A tent in the French camp, near Agincourt*

'Enter the CONSTABLE of FRANCE, the Lord RAM-
BURES, ORLEANS, DAUPHIN, with others'

Constable. Tut! I have the best armour of the world:
would it were day!

Orleans. You have an excellent armour: but let my
horse have his due.

Constable. It is the best horse of Europe.

Orleans. Will it never be morning?

Dauphin. My Lord of Orleans, and my lord high
constable, you talk of horse and armour?

Orleans. You are as well provided of both as any
prince in the world.   10

Dauphin. What a long night is this! I will not change
my horse with any that treads but on four pasterns.
Ça, ha! he bounds from the earth, as if his entrails were
hairs: le cheval volant, the Pegasus, chez les narines de
feu! When I bestride him, I soar, I am a hawk: he trots
the air: the earth sings when he touches it: the basest
horn of his hoof is more musical than the pipe of Hermes.

Orleans. He's of the colour of the nutmeg.

Dauphin. And of the heat of the ginger. It is a beast
for Perseus: he is pure air and fire; and the dull elements 20
of earth and water never appear in him, but only in
patient stillness while his rider mounts him: he is indeed
a horse, and all other jades you may call beasts.

Constable. Indeed, my lord, it is a most absolute and
excellent horse.

Dauphin. It is the prince of palfreys—his neigh is like

the bidding of a monarch, and his countenance enforces homage.

Orleans. No more, cousin.

30 *Dauphin.* Nay, the man hath no wit that cannot, from the rising of the lark to the lodging of the lamb, vary deserved praise on my palfrey: it is a theme as fluent as the sea: turn the sands into eloquent tongues, and my horse is argument for them all: 'tis a subject for a sovereign to reason on, and for a sovereign's sovereign to ride on: and for the world, familiar to us and unknown, to lay apart their particular functions and wonder at him—I once writ a sonnet in his praise, and began thus, "Wonder of nature"—

40 *Orleans.* I have heard a sonnet begin so to one's mistress.

Dauphin. Then did they imitate that which I composed to my courser, for my horse is my mistress.

Orleans. Your mistress bears well.

Dauphin. Me well, which is the prescript praise and perfection of a good and particular mistress.

Constable. Nay, for methought yesterday your mistress shrewdly shook your back.

Dauphin. So perhaps did yours.

50 *Constable.* Mine was not bridled.

Dauphin. O then belike she was old and gentle, and you rode like a kern of Ireland, your French hose off, and in your strait strossers.

Constable. You have good judgement in horsemanship.

Dauphin. Be warned by me then: they that ride so, and ride not warily, fall into foul bogs: I had rather have my horse to my mistress.

Constable. I had as lief have my mistress a jade.

Dauphin. I tell thee, constable, my mistress wears his 60 own hair.

Constable. I could make as true a boast as that, if I had
a sow to my mistress.

Dauphin. "Le chien est retourné à son propre vomisse-
ment, et la truie lavée au bourbier": thou mak'st use of
any thing.

Constable. Yet do I not use my horse for my mistress,
or any such proverb so little kin to the purpose.

Rambures. My lord constable, the armour that I saw
in your tent to-night, are those stars or suns upon it?

Constable. Stars, my lord.　　　　　　　　　　　　　70

Dauphin. Some of them will fall to-morrow, I
hope.

Constable. And yet my sky shall not want.

Dauphin. That may be, for you bear a many super-
fluously, and 'twere more honour some were away.

Constable. Ev'n as your horse bears your praises, who
would trot as well, were some of your brags dismounted.

Dauphin. Would I were able to load him with his
desert! Will it never be day? I will trot to-morrow a
mile, and my way shall be paved with English faces.　　80

Constable. I will not say so, for fear I should be faced
out of my way: but I would it were morning, for I
would fain be about the ears of the English.

Rambures. Who will go to hazard with me for twenty
prisoners?

Constable. You must first go yourself to hazard, ere
you have them.

Dauphin. 'Tis midnight, I'll go arm myself.

> [*he leaves the tent*

Orleans. The Dauphin longs for morning.

Rambures. He longs to eat the English.　　　　　90

Constable. I think he will eat all he kills.

Orleans. By the white hand of my lady, he's a gallant
prince.

Constable. Swear by her foot, that she may tread out the oath.

Orleans. He is simply the most active gentleman of France.

Constable. Doing is activity, and he will still be doing.

Orleans. He never did harm, that I heard of.

100 *Constable.* Nor will do none to-morrow: he will keep that good name still.

Orleans. I know him to be valiant.

Constable. I was told that, by one that knows him better than you.

Orleans. What's he?

Constable. Marry, he told me so himself, and he said he cared not who knew it.

Orleans. He needs not, it is no hidden virtue in him.

Constable. By my faith, sir, but it is: never any body
110 saw it, but his lackey: 'tis a hooded valour, and when it appears, it will bate.

Orleans. Ill will never said well.

Constable. I will cap that proverb with "There is flattery in friendship."

Orleans. And I will take up that with "Give the devil his due."

Constable. Well placed: there stands your friend for the devil: have at the very eye of that proverb with "A pox of the devil."

120 *Orleans.* You are the better at proverbs, by how much "A fool's bolt is soon shot."

Constable. You have shot over.

Orleans. 'Tis not the first time you were overshot.

'*Enter a MESSENGER*'

Messenger. My lord high constable, the English lie within fifteen hundred paces of your tents.

Constable. Who hath measured the ground?

Messenger. The lord Grandpré.

Constable. A valiant and most expert gentleman....
Would it were day! Alas, poor Harry of England! he
longs not for the dawning, as we do.　　　130

Orleans. What a wretched and peevish fellow is this
King of England, to mope with his fat-brained followers
so far out of his knowledge!

Constable. If the English had any apprehension, they
would run away.

Orleans. That they lack: for if their heads had any
intellectual armour, they could never wear such heavy
head-pieces.

Rambures. That island of England breeds very valiant
creatures; their mastiffs are of unmatchable courage.　　　140

Orleans. Foolish curs, that run winking into the mouth
of a Russian bear, and have their heads crushed like
rotten apples! You may as well say, that's a valiant flea
that dare eat his breakfast on the lip of a lion.

Constable. Just, just: and the men do sympathize with
the mastiffs in robustious and rough coming on, leaving
their wits with their wives: and then give them great
meals of beef, and iron and steel; they will eat like
wolves, and fight like devils.

Orleans. Ay, but these English are shrewdly out of 150
beef.

Constable. Then shall we find to-morrow they have
only stomachs to eat, and none to fight....Now is it time
to arm: come, shall we about it?

Orleans. It is now two o'clock: but, let me see, by ten
We shall have each a hundred Englishmen.

　　　　　　　　　　　　　　　　　[they go out

[4. Prologue]

Enter 'CHORUS'

Chorus. Now entertain conjecture of a time
When creeping murmur and the poring dark
Fills the wide vessel of the universe.
From camp to camp, through the foul womb of night
The hum of either army stilly sounds;
That the fixed sentinels almost receive
The secret whispers of each other's watch.
Fire answers fire, and through their paly flames
Each battle sees the other's umbered face.
10 Steed threatens steed, in high and boastful neighs
Piercing the night's dull ear: and from the tents
The armourers, accomplishing the knights,
With busy hammers closing rivets up,
Give dreadful note of preparation.
The country cocks do crow, the clocks do toll,
And the third hour of drowsy morning name.
Proud of their numbers, and secure in soul,
The confident and over-lusty French
Do the low-rated English play at dice;
20 And chide the cripple tardy-gaited night,
Who like a foul and ugly witch doth limp
So tediously away. The poor condemnéd English,
Like sacrifices, by their watchful fires
Sit patiently, and inly ruminate
The morning's danger: and their gesture sad,
Investing lank-lean cheeks, and war-worn coats,
Presenteth them unto the gazing moon
So many horrid ghosts. O now, who will behold
The royal captain of this ruined band
30 Walking from watch to watch, from tent to tent,

Let him cry, "Praise and glory on his head!"
For forth he goes, and visits all his host,
Bids them good morrow with a modest smile,
And calls them brothers, friends, and countrymen.
Upon his royal face there is no note,
How dread an army hath enrounded him;
Nor doth he dedicate one jot of colour
Unto the weary and all-watchéd night:
But freshly looks, and over-bears attaint
With cheerful semblance, and sweet majesty: 40
That every wretch, pining and pale before,
Beholding him, plucks comfort from his looks.
A largess universal, like the sun,
His liberal eye doth give to every one,
Thawing cold fear, that mean and gentle all
Behold, as may unworthiness define,
A little touch of Harry in the night.
And so our scene must to the battle fly:
Where—O for pity!—we shall much disgrace,
With four or five most vile and ragged foils,   50
Right ill-disposed, in brawl ridiculous,
The name of Agincourt: yet sit and see,
Minding true things by what their mock'ries be.

['*Exit*'

[4. 1.] *A passage between the tents of the English camp*
at Agincourt. Before dawn

King HENRY, BEDFORD, and GLOUCESTER

King Henry. Gloucester, 'tis true that we are in
    great danger,
The greater therefore should our courage be....
Good morrow, brother Bedford...God Almighty!

There is some soul of goodness in things evil,
Would men observingly distil it out.
For our bad neighbour makes us early stirrers,
Which is both healthful, and good husbandry.
Besides, they are our outward consciences
And preachers to us all, admonishing
10 That we should dress us fairly for our end.
Thus may we gather honey from the weed,
And make a moral of the devil himself.

Erpingham comes up

Good morrow, old Sir Thomas Erpingham:
A good soft pillow for that good white head
Were better than a churlish turf of France.
   Erpingham. Not so, my liege—this lodging likes
      me better,
Since I may say 'Now lie I like a king.'
   King Henry. 'Tis good for men to love their
      present pains,
Upon example—so the spirit is eased:
20 And when the mind is quickened, out of doubt
The organs, though defunct and dead before,
Break up their drowsy grave, and newly move
With casted slough and fresh legerity....
Lend me thy cloak, Sir Thomas...Brothers both,
Commend me to the princes in our camp;
Do my good morrow to them, and anon
Desire them all to my pavilion.
   Gloucester. We shall, my liege.
   Erpingham. Shall I attend your grace?
   King Henry.   No, my good knight:
30 Go with my brothers to my lords of England:
I and my bosom must debate awhile,
And then I would no other company.

Erpingham.　The Lord in heaven bless thee,
　　noble Harry!
King Henry.　God-a-mercy, old heart! thou
　　speak'st cheerfully.　　[*they take leave of the King*

PISTOL *steals into view, is about to pilfer from a tent,
　　but starts as he perceives someone in the dark*

Pistol.　Qui va là?
King Henry.　A friend.
Pistol.　Discuss unto me, art thou officer,
Or art thou base, common, and popular?
King Henry.　I am a gentleman of a company.
Pistol.　Trail'st thou the puissant pike?　　　　40
King Henry.　Even so: what are you?
Pistol.　As good a gentleman as the emperor.
King Henry.　Then you are a better than the king.
Pistol.　The king's a bawcock, and a heart of gold,
A lad of life, an imp of Fame,
Of parents good, of fist most valiant:
I kiss his dirty shoe, and from heart-string
I love the lovely bully....What is thy name?
King Henry.　Harry le Roy.
Pistol.　Le Roy? a Cornish name: art thou of　　50
　　Cornish crew?
King Henry.　No, I am a Welshman.
Pistol.　Know'st thou Fluellen?
King Henry.　Yes.
Pistol.　Tell him I'll knock his leek about his pate
Upon Saint Davy's day.
King Henry.　Do not you wear your dagger in your
cap that day, lest he knock that about yours.
Pistol.　Art thou his friend?
King Henry.　And his kinsman too.
Pistol.　The figo for thee then!　　　　60

King Henry. I thank you: God be with you!
Pistol. My name is Pistol called.　　　　　　*[he goes*
King Henry. It sorts well with your fierceness.

*The King withdraws a little; FLUELLEN and GOWER
encounter, coming different ways.*

Gower. Captain Fluellen!
Fluellen. So! in the name of Jesu Christ, speak fewer...
It is the greatest admiration in the universal world, when
the true and ancient prerogatifes and laws of the wars
is not kept: if you would take the pains but to examine
the wars of Pompey the Great, you shall find, I warrant
70 you, that there is no tiddle taddle nor pibble pabble in
Pompey's camp: I warrant you, you shall find the
ceremonies of the wars, and the cares of it, and the forms
of it, and the sobriety of it, and the modesty of it, to be
otherwise.
Gower. Why, the enemy is loud, you hear him all
night.
Fluellen. If the enemy is an ass and a fool, and a prating
coxcomb, is it meet, think you, that we should also, look
you, be an ass and a fool, and a prating coxcomb? in
80 your own conscience now?
Gower. I will speak lower.
Fluellen. I pray you, and beseech you, that you will.
　　　　　　　　　　　　　　　　[they depart severally
King Henry. Though it appear a little out of fashion,
There is much care and valour in this Welshman.

*'Three soldiers, JOHN BATES, ALEXANDER COURT,
and MICHAEL WILLIAMS,' come up*

Court. Brother John Bates, is not that the morning
which breaks yonder?

Bates. I think it be: but we have no great cause to desire the approach of day.

Williams. We see yonder the beginning of the day, but I think we shall never see the end of it....Who goes 90 there?

King Henry. A friend.

Williams. Under what captain serve you?

King Henry. Under Sir Thomas Erpingham.

Williams. A good old commander, and a most kind gentleman: I pray you, what thinks he of our estate?

King Henry. Even as men wracked upon a sand, that look to be washed off the next tide.

Bates. He hath not told his thought to the king?

King Henry. No: nor it is not meet he should: for, 100 though I speak it to you, I think the king is but a man, as I am: the violet smells to him as it doth to me; the element shows to him as it doth to me; all his senses have but human conditions: his ceremonies laid by, in his nakedness he appears but a man; and though his affections are higher mounted than ours, yet, when they stoop, they stoop with the like wing: therefore, when he sees reason of fears, as we do, his fears, out of doubt, be of the same relish as ours are: yet, in reason, no man should possess him with any appearance of fear, lest he, 110 by showing it, should dishearten his army.

Bates. He may show what outward courage he will: but I believe, as cold a night as 'tis, he could wish himself in Thames up to the neck; and so I would he were, and I by him, at all adventures, so we were quit here.

King Henry. By my troth, I will speak my conscience of the king: I think he would not wish himself any where but where he is.

Bates. Then I would he were here alone; so should 120

he be sure to be ransomed, and a many poor men's lives saved.

King Henry. I dare say you love him not so ill, to wish him here alone: howsoever you speak this to feel other men's minds. Methinks I could not die any where so contented as in the king's company; his cause being just, and his quarrel honourable.

Williams. That's more than we know.

Bates. Ay, or more than we should seek after; for we 130 know enough, if we know we are the king's subjects: if his cause be wrong, our obedience to the king wipes the crime of it out of us.

Williams. But if the cause be not good, the king himself hath a heavy reckoning to make, when all those legs, and arms, and heads, chopped off in a battle, shall join together at the latter day, and cry all "We died at such a place"; some swearing, some crying for a surgeon; some upon their wives, left poor behind them; some upon the debts they owe; some upon their children rawly 140 left…I am afeard there are few die well, that die in a battle: for how can they charitably dispose of any thing, when blood is their argument? Now, if these men do not die well, it will be a black matter for the king, that led them to it; who to disobey were against all proportion of subjection.

King Henry. So, if a son that is by his father sent about merchandise do sinfully miscarry upon the sea, the imputation of his wickedness, by your rule, should be imposed upon his father that sent him: or if a servant, 150 under his master's command, transporting a sum of money, be assailed by robbers, and die in many irreconciled iniquities, you may call the business of the master the author of the servant's damnation…But this is not so: the king is not bound to answer the particular endings

of his soldiers, the father of his son, nor the master of his
servant; for they purpose not their death, when they
purpose their services. Besides, there is no king, be his
cause never so spotless, if it come to the arbitrement of
swords, can try it out with all unspotted soldiers: some,
peradventure, have on them the guilt of premeditated 160
and contrived murder; some, of beguiling virgins with
the broken seals of perjury; some, making the wars their
bulwark, that have before gored the gentle bosom of
peace with pillage and robbery. Now, if these men have
defeated the law, and outrun native punishment, though
they can outstrip men, they have no wings to fly from
God. War is His beadle, war is His vengeance: so that
here men are punished, for before breach of the king's
laws, in now the king's quarrel: where they feared the
death, they have borne life away; and where they would 170
be safe, they perish. Then if they die unprovided, no
more is the king guilty of their damnation than he was
before guilty of those impieties for the which they are
now visited. Every subject's duty is the king's, but every
subject's soul is his own. Therefore should every soldier
in the wars do as every sick man in his bed, wash every
mote out of his conscience: and dying so, death is to him
advantage; or not dying, the time was blessedly lost,
wherein such preparation was gained: and in him that
escapes, it were not sin to think that, making God so free 180
an offer, He let him outlive that day, to see His greatness,
and to teach others how they should prepare.

Williams. 'Tis certain, every man that dies ill, the ill
upon his own head, the king is not to answer it.

Bates. I do not desire he should answer for me, and
yet I determine to fight lustily for him.

King Henry. I myself heard the king say he would not
be ransomed.

Williams. Ay, he said so, to make us fight cheerfully:
190 but when our throats are cut, he may be ransomed, and
we ne'er the wiser.

King Henry. If I live to see it, I will never trust his
word after.

Williams. You pay him then! That's a perilous shot
out of an elder-gun, that a poor and a private displeasure
can do against a monarch! you may as well go about to
turn the sun to ice, with fanning in his face with a
peacock's feather...You'll never trust his word after!
come, 'tis a foolish saying.

200 *King Henry.* Your reproof is something too round—
I should be angry with you, if the time were convenient.

Williams. Let it be a quarrel between us, if you live.

King Henry. I embrace it.

Williams. How shall I know thee again?

King Henry. Give me any gage of thine, and I will
wear it in my bonnet: then, if ever thou dar'st acknowledge it, I will make it my quarrel.

Williams. Here's my glove: give me another of thine.

King Henry. There.

210 *Williams.* This will I also wear in my cap: if ever
thou come to me and say, after to-morrow, "This is my
glove", by this hand I will take thee a box on the ear.

King Henry. If ever I live to see it, I will challenge it.

Williams. Thou dar'st as well be hanged.

King Henry. Well, I will do it, though I take thee in
the king's company.

Williams. Keep thy word: fare thee well.

Bates. Be friends, you English fools, be friends; we
have French quarrels enow, if you could tell how to
220 reckon.

King Henry. Indeed, the French may lay twenty
French crowns to one, they will beat us, for they bear

them on their shoulders: but it is no English treason to
cut French crowns, and to-morrow the king himself will
be a clipper.   [*the soldiers go their way*
Upon the king! let us our lives, our souls,
Our debts, our careful wives,
Our children, and our sins, lay on the king!
We must bear all. O hard condition,
Twin-born with greatness, subject to the breath   230
Of every fool, whose sense no more can feel
But his own wringing! What infinite heart's ease
Must kings neglect that private men enjoy!
And what have kings, that privates have not too,
Save Ceremony, save general Ceremony?
And what art thou, thou idol Ceremony?
What kind of god art thou, that suffer'st more
Of mortal griefs than do thy worshippers?
What are thy rents? what are thy comings in?
O Ceremony, show me but thy worth!   240
What! Is thy soul of adoration?
Art thou aught else but place, degree, and form,
Creating awe and fear in other men?
Wherein thou art less happy, being feared,
Than they in fearing.
What drink'st thou oft, instead of homage sweet,
But poisoned flattery? O, be sick, great greatness,
And bid thy ceremony give thee cure!
Thinkst thou the fiery fever will go out
With titles blown from adulation?   250
Will it give place to flexure and low bending?
Canst thou, when thou command'st the beggar's knee,
Command the health of it? No, thou proud dream,
That play'st so subtly with a king's repose.
I am a king that find thee: and I know,
'Tis not the balm, the sceptre, and the ball,

The sword, the mace, the crown imperial,
The intertissued robe of gold and pearl,
The farcéd title running 'fore the king,
260 The throne he sits on: nor the tide of pomp
That beats upon the high shore of this world:
No, not all these, thrice-gorgeous ceremony,
Not all these, laid in bed majestical,
Can sleep so soundly as the wretched slave:
Who, with a body filled, and vacant mind,
Gets him to rest, crammed with distressful bread,
Never sees horrid night, the child of hell:
But, like a lackey, from the rise to set,
Sweats in the eye of Phœbus; and all night
270 Sleeps in Elysium: next day, after dawn,
Doth rise, and help Hyperion to his horse,
And follows so the ever-running year
With profitable labour to his grave:
And, but for ceremony, such a wretch,
Winding up days with toil, and nights with sleep,
Had the fore-hand and vantage of a king.
The slave, a member of the country's peace,
Enjoys it; but in gross brain little wots
What watch the king keeps to maintain the peace,
280 Whose hours the peasant best advantages.

ERPINGHAM returns

Erpingham. My lord, your nobles, jealous of
        your absence,
Seek through your camp to find you.
    King Henry.   Good old knight,
Collect them all together at my tent:
I'll be before thee.
    Erpingham.   I shall do't, my lord.   [*he goes*
    King Henry. [*kneels apart*] O God of battles, steel my
        soldiers' hearts,

Possess them not with fear: take from them now
†The sense of reck'ning, or th'opposéd numbers
Pluck their hearts from them. Not to-day, O Lord,
O not to-day, think not upon the fault
My father made in compassing the crown!   290
I Richard's body have interréd new,
And on it have bestowed more contrite tears,
Than from it issued forcéd drops of blood.
Five hundred poor I have in yearly pay,
Who twice a day their withered hands hold up
Toward heaven, to pardon blood: and I have built
Two chantries, where the sad and solemn priests
Sing still for Richard's soul. More will I do:
Though all that I can do is nothing worth;
Since that my penitence comes after all,   300
Imploring pardon.   [*he continues in prayer*

    GLOUCESTER *returns calling*

  Gloucester. My liege!
  King Henry. [*rises*] My brother Gloucester's voice?
Ay:
I know thy errand, I will go with thee:
The day, my friends, and all things stay for me.
                              [*they go together*

[4. 2.]   *A tent in the French camp (as before); daybreak*

    The DAUPHIN, ORLEANS, RAMBURES, *and others,*
                      awaking

  Orleans. The sun doth gild our armour. Up, my lords!
  Dauphin. Montez à cheval! My horse! varlet!
laquais! ha!
  Orleans. O brave spirit!
  Dauphin. Via! les eaux et la terre!

Orleans. Rien puis? l'air et le feu?
Dauphin. Ciel! cousin Orleans.

Constable *enters*

               Now, my lord Constable?
Constable. Hark how our steeds for present
    service neigh.
Dauphin. Mount them, and make incision in
    their hides,
10 That their hot blood may spin in English eyes,
And dout them with superfluous courage, ha!
    Rambures. What, will you have them weep our
    horses' blood?
How shall we then behold their natural tears?

'Enter Messenger'

Messenger. The English are embattled, you
    French peers.
Constable. To horse, you gallant princes, straight
    to horse!
Do but behold yon poor and starvéd band,
And your fair show shall suck away their souls,
Leaving them but the shales and husks of men.
There is not work enough for all our hands,
20 Scarce blood enough in all their sickly veins,
To give each naked curtle-axe a stain,
That our French gallants shall to-day draw out,
And sheathe for lack of sport. Let us but blow on them,
The vapour of our valour will o'erturn them.
'Tis positive 'gainst all exceptions, lords,
That our superfluous lackeys, and our peasants,
Who in unnecessary action swarm
About our squares of battle, were enow
To purge this field of such a hilding foe;

Though we upon this mountain's basis by   30
Took stand for idle speculation:
But that our honours must not. What's to say?
A very little little let us do,
And all is done...Then let the trumpets sound
The tucket sonance, and the note to mount:
For our approach shall so much dare the field,
That England shall couch down in fear, and yield.

'*Enter GRANDPRÉ*'

Grandpré. Why do you stay so long, my lords
    of France?
Yon island carrions, desperate of their bones,
Ill-favouredly become the morning field: 40
Their ragged curtains poorly are let loose,
And our air shakes them passing scornfully.
Big Mars seems bankrout in their beggared host,
And faintly through a rusty beaver peeps.
The horsemen sit like fixéd candlesticks,
With torch-staves in their hand: and their poor jades
Lob down their heads, dropping the hides and hips,
The gum down-roping from their pale-dead eyes,
And in their pale dull mouths the gimmaled bit
Lies foul with chawed-grass, still and motionless.   50
And their executors, the knavish crows,
Fly o'er them all, impatient for their hour.
Description cannot suit itself in words,
To demonstrate the life of such a battle,
In life so lifeless as it shows itself.
    Constable. They have said their prayers, and they stay
        for death.
    Dauphin. Shall we go send them dinners, and
        fresh suits,
And give their fasting horses provender,

And after fight with them?
60 *Constable.* I stay but for my guidon: to the field!
I will the banner from a trumpet take,
And use it for my haste....Come, come away!
The sun is high, and we outwear the day.

[*they hurry forth*

[4. 3.] *The English camp; before the King's pavilion*

'*Enter* GLOUCESTER, BEDFORD, EXETER, ERPINGHAM
with all his host: SALISBURY *and* WESTMORELAND,'
with others

Gloucester. Where is the king?
Bedford. The king himself is rode to view their battle.
Westmoreland. Of fighting men they have full three-
score thousand.
Exeter. There's five to one, besides they all are fresh.
Salisbury. God's arm strike with us! 'tis a
fearful odds....
God bye you, princes all; I'll to my charge:
If we no more meet till we meet in heaven,
Then joyfully, my noble Lord of Bedford,
My dear Lord Gloucester, and my good Lord Exeter,
10 And my kind kinsman, warriors all, adieu!
Bedford. Farewell, good Salisbury, and good luck go
with thee!
Exeter. Farewell, kind lord: fight valiantly to-day:
And yet I do thee wrong, to mind thee of it,
For thou art framed of the firm truth of valour.

[*Salisbury goes*

Bedford. He is as full of valour as of kindness,
Princely in both.

The King approaches

  Westmoreland.   O that we now had here
But one ten thousand of those men in England,
That do no work to-day!
  King Henry.   What's he that wishes so?
My cousin Westmoreland? No, my fair cousin:
If we are marked to die, we are enow   20
To do our country loss: and if to live,
The fewer men, the greater share of honour.
God's will, I pray thee wish not one man more.
By Jove, I am not covetous for gold,
Nor care I who doth feed upon my cost:
It earns me not if men my garments wear;
Such outward things dwell not in my desires.
But if it be a sin to covet honour,
I am the most offending soul alive.
No, faith, my coz, wish not a man from England: 30
God's peace, I would not lose so great an honour,
As one man more, methinks, would share from me,
For the best hope I have. O, do not wish one more:
Rather proclaim it, Westmoreland, through my host,
That he which hath no stomach to this fight,
Let him depart, his passport shall be made,
And crowns for convoy put into his purse:
We would not die in that man's company
That fears his fellowship, to die with us.
This day is called the feast of Crispian: 40
He that outlives this day, and comes safe home,
Will stand a tip-toe when this day is named,
And rouse him at the name of Crispian.
He that shall see this day, and live old age,
Will yearly on the vigil feast his neighbours,
And say, "To-morrow is Saint Crispian."

Then will he strip his sleeve, and show his scars,
And say, "These wounds I had on Crispin's day."
Old men forget; yet all shall be forgot,
50 But he'll remember, with advantages,
What feats he did that day. Then shall our names,
Familiar in his mouth as household words,
Harry the king, Bedford and Exeter,
Warwick and Talbot, Salisbury and Gloucester,
Be in their flowing cups freshly remembered.
This story shall the good man teach his son:
And Crispin Crispian shall ne'er go by,
From this day to the ending of the world,
But we in it shall be rememberéd;
60 We few, we happy few, we band of brothers:
For he to-day that sheds his blood with me
Shall be my brother: be he ne'er so vile,
This day shall gentle his condition.
And gentlemen in England, now a-bed,
Shall think themselves accursed they were not here;
And hold their manhoods cheap, whiles any speaks
That fought with us upon Saint Crispin's day.

SALISBURY returns

   Salisbury. My sovereign lord, bestow yourself
     with speed:
The French are bravely in their battles set,
70 And will with all expedience charge on us.
   King Henry. All things are ready, if our minds be so.
   Westmoreland. Perish the man whose mind is
     backward now!
   King Henry. Thou dost not wish more help from
     England, coz?
   Westmoreland. God's will, my liege, would you and
     I alone,

Without more help, could fight this royal battle!
 King Henry. Why, now thou hast unwished five
  thousand men:
Which likes me better than to wish us one....
You know your places: God be with you all!

  A 'tucket' sounds and MONTJOY *approaches*

 Montjoy. Once more I come to know of thee,
  King Harry,
If for thy ransom thou wilt now compound,   80
Before thy most assuréd overthrow:
For certainly thou art so near the gulf,
Thou needs must be englutted. Besides, in mercy,
The Constable desires thee thou wilt mind
Thy followers of repentance; that their souls
May make a peaceful and a sweet retire
From off these fields: where, wretches, their poor bodies
Must lie and fester.
 King Henry.   Who hath sent thee now?
 Montjoy. The Constable of France.
 King Henry. I pray thee bear my former answer back: 90
Bid them achieve me, and then sell my bones.
Good God! why should they mock poor fellows thus?
The man that once did sell the lion's skin
While the beast lived, was killed with hunting him.
A many of our bodies shall no doubt
Find native graves: upon the which, I trust,
Shall witness live in brass of this day's work.
And those that leave their valiant bones in France,
Dying like men, though buried in your dunghills,
They shall be famed: for there the sun shall greet them, 100
And draw their honours reeking up to heaven,
Leaving their earthly parts to choke your clime,
The smell whereof shall breed a plague in France.

Mark then abounding valour in our English:
That being dead, like to the bullet's crasing,
Break out into a second course of mischief,
Killing in relapse of mortality....
Let me speak proudly: tell the Constable
We are but warriors for the working-day:
110 Our gayness and our gilt are all besmirched
With rainy marching in the painful field.
There's not a piece of feather in our host—
Good argument, I hope, we will not fly—
And time hath worn us into slovenry.
But, by the mass, our hearts are in the trim:
And my poor soldiers tell me, yet ere night
They'll be in fresher robes, or they will pluck
The gay new coats o'er the French soldiers' heads,
And turn them out of service. If they do this—
120 As, if God please, they shall—my ransom then
Will soon be levied. Herald, save thou thy labour:
Come thou no more for ransom, gentle herald,
They shall have none, I swear, but these my joints:
Which if they have, as I will leave 'em them,
Shall yield them little, tell the Constable.
    Montjoy. I shall, King Harry. And so fare thee well:
Thou never shalt hear herald any more.   [*he goes*
    King Henry. I fear thou wilt once more come again
for a ransom.

The Duke of YORK *comes up*

130 *York.* My lord, most humbly on my knee I beg
The leading of the vaward.
    King Henry. Take it, brave York....Now soldiers,
        march away,
And how thou pleasest, God, dispose the day!
                            [*the host marches forward*

[4. 4.]   *Near the field of battle*

'*Alarum. Excursions. Enter* PISTOL,
FRENCH SOLDIER,' *and* 'BOY'

Pistol. Yield, cur!

French Soldier. Je pense que vous êtes le gentilhomme
de bonne qualité.

Pistol. Qualtitie! Calen o custure me! Art thou a
gentleman? what is thy name? discuss.

French Soldier. O Seigneur Dieu!

Pistol. O, Signieur Dew should be a gentleman:
Perpend my words, O Signieur Dew, and mark:
O Signieur Dew, thou diest on point of fox,
Except, O signieur, thou do give to me   10
Egregious ransom.

French Soldier. O, prenez miséricorde! ayez pitié de
moi!

Pistol. Moy shall not serve, I will have forty moys:
Or I will fetch thy rim out at thy throat,
In drops of crimson blood.

French Soldier. Est-il impossible d'échapper la force
de ton bras?

Pistol. Brass, cur?
Thou damnéd and luxurious mountain goat,   20
Offer'st me brass?

French Soldier. O pardonnez moi!

Pistol. Say'st thou me so? is that a ton of moys?
Come hither, boy, ask me this slave in French
What is his name.

Boy. Écoutez: comment êtes-vous appelé?

French Soldier. Monsieur le Fer.

Boy. He says his name is Master Fer.

Pistol. Master Fer! I'll fer him, and firk him, and
ferret him: discuss the same in French unto him.   30

Boy. I do not know the French for *fer*, and *ferret*, and *firk*.

Pistol. Bid him prepare, for I will cut his throat.

French Soldier. Que dit-il, monsieur?

Boy. Il me commande à vous dire que vous faites vous prêt, car ce soldat ici est disposé tout à cette heure de couper votre gorge.

Pistol. Owy, cuppele gorge, permafoy,
Peasant, unless thou give me crowns, brave crowns;
40 Or mangled shalt thou be by this my sword.

French Soldier. O, je vous supplie, pour l'amour de Dieu, me pardonner! Je suis le gentilhomme de bonne maison, gardez ma vie, et je vous donnerai deux cents écus.

Pistol. What are his words?

Boy. He prays you to save his life, he is a gentleman of a good house, and for his ransom he will give you two hundred crowns.

Pistol. Tell him my fury shall abate, and I
50 The crowns will take.

French Soldier. Petit monsieur, que dit-il?

Boy. Encore qu'il est contre son jurement de pardonner aucun prisonnier: néanmoins, pour les écus que vous l'avez promis, il est content à vous donner la liberté, le franchisement.

French Soldier. Sur mes genoux je vous donne mille remercîments, et je m'estime heureux que je suis tombé entre les mains d'un chevalier, je pense, le plus brave, vaillant, et très distingué seigneur d'Angleterre.

60 *Pistol.* Expound unto me, boy.

Boy. He gives you upon his knees a thousand thanks, and he esteems himself happy that he hath fallen into the hands of one, as he thinks, the most brave, valorous, and thrice-worthy signieur of England.

Pistol. As I suck blood, I will some mercy show.
Follow me!   [*Pistol passes in*
Boy. Suivez-vous le grand capitaine!
                    [*the French soldier follows*
I did never know so full a voice issue from so empty
a heart: but the saying is true, "The empty vessel makes
the greatest sound." Bardolph and Nym had ten times 70
more valour than this roaring devil i'th'old play, that
every one may pare his nails with a wooden dagger, and
they are both hanged, and so would this be, if he durst
steal any thing adventurously....I must stay with the
lackeys with the luggage of our camp; the French might
have a good prey of us, if he knew of it, for there is none
to guard it but boys.   [*he goes*

[4. 5.] '*Enter* CONSTABLE, ORLEANS, BOURBON,
          DAUPHIN, *and* RAMBURES' *in flight*

Constable. O diable!
Orleans. O Seigneur! le jour est perdu, tout est perdu!
Dauphin. Mort Dieu! ma vie! all is confounded, all!
Reproach and everlasting shame
Sits mocking in our plumes.   ['*a short alarum*'
O méchante fortune! Do not run away.
Constable. Why, all our ranks are broke.
Dauphin. O perdurable shame! let's stab ourselves:
Be these the wretches that we played at dice for?
Orleans. Is this the king we sent to for his ransom? 10
Bourbon. Shame, and eternal shame, nothing but
          shame!
†Let us die in harness: once more back again,
And he that will not follow Bourbon now,
Let him go hence, and with his cap in hand
Like a base pandar hold the chamber-door,
Whilst by a slave, no gentler than my dog,

His fairest daughter is contaminated.

Constable. Disorder, that hath spoiled us, friend
us now!

Let us on heaps go offer up our lives.

20 *Orleans.* We are enow yet living in the field
To smother up the English in our throngs,
If any order might be thought upon.

Bourbon. The devil take order now! I'll to the throng;
Let life be short, else shame will be too long.

                                 [they return to the field

    [4. 6.] '*Alarum. Enter the King and his train,
          with prisoners,*' EXETER *and others*

King Henry. Well have we done, thrice-
valiant countrymen,

But all's not done—yet keep the French the field.

Exeter. The Duke of York commends him to
your majesty.

King Henry. Lives he, good uncle? thrice within
this hour

I saw him down; thrice up again, and fighting,
From helmet to the spur all blood he was.

Exeter. In which array, brave soldier, doth he lie,
Larding the plain: and by his bloody side,
Yoke-fellow to his honour-owing wounds,

10 The noble Earl of Suffolk also lies.
Suffolk first died, and York, all haggled over,
Comes to him, where in gore he lay insteeped,
And takes him by the beard, kisses the gashes
That bloodily did yawn upon his face,
And cries aloud, 'Tarry, my cousin Suffolk!
My soul shall thine keep company to heaven:
Tarry, sweet soul, for mine, then fly abreast:
As in this glorious and well-foughten field

We kept together in our chivalry.'
Upon these words I came, and cheered him up,   20
He smiled me in the face, raught me his hand,
And, with a feeble gripe, says, 'Dear my lord,
Commend my service to my sovereign.'
So did he turn, and over Suffolk's neck
He threw his wounded arm, and kissed his lips,
And so espoused to death, with blood he sealed
A testament of noble-ending love:
The pretty and sweet manner of it forced
Those waters from me which I would have stopped,
But I had not so much of man in me,   30
And all my mother came into mine eyes,
And gave me up to tears.
King Henry.   I blame you not,
For, hearing this, I must perforce compound
With mistful eyes, or they will issue too....   ['*alarum*'
But hark! what new alarum is this same?
The French have reinforced their scattered men:
Then every soldier kill his prisoners,
Give the word through.   [*they hasten forward*

[4. 7.]   '*Enter FLUELLEN and GOWER*'

Fluellen. Kill the poys and the luggage! 'tis expressly
against the law of arms, 'tis as arrant a piece of knavery,
mark you now, as can be offert. In your conscience
now, is it not?

Gower. 'Tis certain there's not a boy left alive, and
the cowardly rascals that ran from the battle ha' done
this slaughter: besides, they have burned and carried
away all that was in the king's tent, wherefore the king
most worthily hath caused every soldier to cut his
prisoner's throat. O, 'tis a gallant king!   10

Fluellen. Ay, he was porn at Monmouth, Captain

Gower: what call you the town's name where Alexander the pig was born?

Gower. Alexander the Great.

Fluellen. Why, I pray you, is not pig great? The pig, or the great, or the mighty, or the huge, or the magnanimous, are all one reckonings, save the phrase is a little variations.

Gower. I think Alexander the Great was born in
20 Macedon, his father was called Philip of Macedon, as I take it.

Fluellen. I think it is in Macedon where Alexander is porn: I tell you, captain, if you look in the maps of the 'orld, I warrant you sall find, in the comparisons between Macedon and Monmouth, that the situations, look you, is both alike. There is a river in Macedon, and there is also moreover a river at Monmouth, it is called Wye at Monmouth: but it is out of my prains what is the name of the other river: but 'tis all one, 'tis
30 alike as my fingers is to my fingers, and there is salmons in both. If you mark Alexander's life well, Harry of Monmouth's life is come after it indifferent well, for there is figures in all things. Alexander, God knows, and you know, in his rages, and his furies, and his wraths, and his cholers, and his moods, and his displeasures, and his indignations, and also being a little intoxicates in his prains, did in his ales and his angers, look you, kill his best friend Cleitus.

Gower. Our king is not like him in that, he never killed
40 any of his friends.

Fluellen. It is not well done, mark you now, to take the tales out of my mouth, ere it is made and finished. I speak but in the figures and comparisons of it: as Alexander killed his friend Cleitus, being in his ales and his cups; so also Harry Monmouth, being in his right

wits and his good judgements, turned away the fat
knight with the great-belly doublet: he was full of jests,
and gipes, and knaveries, and mocks, I have forgot his
name.

Gower. Sir John Falstaff.   50

Fluellen. That is he: I'll tell you, there is good men
porn at Monmouth.

Gower. Here comes his majesty.

'*Alarum. Enter King HARRY and BOURBON with
prisoners,' meeting WARWICK, GLOUCESTER, EXETER,
heralds and soldiers, WILLIAMS among them. 'Flourish.*'

King Henry. I was not angry since I came to France
Until this instant....Take a trumpet, herald,
Ride thou unto the horsemen on yon hill:
If they will fight with us, bid them come down,
Or void the field: they do offend our sight.
If they'll do neither, we will come to them,
And make them skirr away, as swift as stones   60
Enforcéd from the old Assyrian slings:
Besides, we'll cut the throats of those we have,
And not a man of them that we shall take
Shall taste our mercy....Go and tell them so.

                                    [*an English herald obeys*

                    MONTJOY *approaches*

Exeter. Here comes the herald of the French, my
    liege.

Gloucester. His eyes are humbler than they used to be.

King Henry. How now, what means this, herald?
    Know'st thou not
That I have fined these bones of mine for ransom?
Com'st thou again for ransom?

Montjoy.   No, great king:

70 I come to thee for charitable licence,
That we may wander o'er this bloody field,
To book our dead, and then to bury them,
To sort our nobles fróm our common men.
For many of our princes—woe the while!—
Lie drowned and soaked in mercenary blood:
So do our vulgar drench their peasant limbs
In blood of princes, and their wounded steeds
Fret fetlock deep in gore, and with wild rage
Yerk out their arméd heels at their dead masters,
80 Killing them twice....O, give us leave, great king,
To view the field in safety, and dispose
Of their dead bodies.

   King Henry.   I tell thee truly, herald,
I know not if the day be ours or no,
For yet a many of your horsemen peer,
And gallop o'er the field.

   Montjoy.   The day is yours.

   King Henry. Praiséd be God, and not our strength,
    for it!
What is this castle called that stands hard by?

   Montjoy. They call it Agincourt.

   King Henry. Then call we this the field of Agincourt,
90 Fought on the day of Crispin Crispianus.

   Fluellen. Your grandfather of famous memory, an't
please your majesty, and your great-uncle Edward the
Plack Prince of Wales, as I have read in the chronicles,
fought a most prave pattle here in France.

   King Henry. They did, Fluellen.

   Fluellen. Your majesty says very true: if your majesties
is remembered of it, the Welshmen did good service in
a garden where leeks did grow, wearing leeks in their
Monmouth caps, which your majesty know to this hour
100 is an honourable badge of the service: and I do believe

your majesty takes no scorn to wear the leek upon Saint Tavy's day.

King Henry. I wear it for a memorable honour: For I am Welsh, you know, good countryman.

Fluellen. All the water in Wye cannot wash your majesty's Welsh plood out of your pody, I can tell you that: God pless it, and preserve it, as long as it pleases his grace, and his majesty too!

King Henry. Thanks, good my countryman.

Fluellen. By Jeshu, I am your majesty's countryman, 110 I care not who know it: I will confess it to all the 'orld, I need not to be ashamed of your majesty, praised be God, so long as your majesty is an honest man.

King Henry. God keep me so! Our heralds go
     with him,
Bring me just notice of the numbers dead
On both our parts....[*heralds depart with Montjoy*
     Call yonder fellow hither.. [*he points to Williams*

Exeter. Soldier, you must come to the king.

King Henry. Soldier, why wear'st thou that glove in thy cap?

Williams. An't please your majesty, 'tis the gage of 120 one that I should fight withal, if he be alive.

King Henry. An Englishman?

Williams. An't please your majesty, a rascal that swaggered with me last night: who, if a' live and ever dare to challenge this glove, I have sworn to take him a box o'th'ear: or if I can see my glove in his cap—which he swore, as he was a soldier, he would wear if alive— I will strike it out soundly.

King Henry. What think you, Captain Fluellen, is it fit this soldier keep his oath?   130

Fluellen. He is a craven and a villain else, an't please your majesty, in my conscience.

King Henry. It may be his enemy is a gentleman of great sort, quite from the answer of his degree.

Fluellen. Though he be as good a gentleman as the devil is, as Lucifer and Belzebub himself, it is necessary, look your grace, that he keep his vow and his oath: if he be perjured, see you now, his reputation is as arrant a villain and a Jack-sauce as ever his black shoe trod upon
140 God's ground and his earth, in my conscience, la!

King Henry. Then keep thy vow, sirrah, when thou meet'st the fellow.

Williams. So I will, my liege, as I live.

King Henry. Who serv'st thou under?

Williams. Under Captain Gower, my liege.

Fluellen. Gower is a good captain, and is good knowledge and literatured in the wars.

King Henry. Call him hither to me, soldier.

Williams. I will, my liege.   [*he goes*
150 *King Henry.* Here, Fluellen, wear thou this favour for me, and stick it in thy cap: when Alençon and myself were down together, I plucked this glove from his helm: if any man challenge this, he is a friend to Alençon, and an enemy to our person; if thou encounter any such, apprehend him, an thou dost me love.

Fluellen. Your grace does me as great honours as can be desired in the hearts of his subjects: I would fain see the man that has but two legs that shall find himself aggriefed at this glove; that is all: but I would fain
160 see it once, an please God of his grace that I might see.

King Henry. Know'st thou Gower?

Fluellen. He is my dear friend, an please you.

King Henry. Pray thee, go seek him, and bring him to my tent.

Fluellen. I will fetch him.   [*he goes*

King Henry. My Lord of Warwick, and my
    brother Gloucester,
Follow Fluellen closely at the heels.
The glove which I have given him for a favour
May haply purchase him a box o'th'ear.   170
It is the soldier's: I by bargain should
Wear it myself. Follow, good cousin Warwick:
If that the soldier strike him, as I judge
By his blunt bearing he will keep his word,
Some sudden mischief may arise of it:
For I do know Fluellen valiant,
And, touched with choler, hot as gunpowder,
And quickly will return an injury.
Follow, and see there be no harm between them....
Go you with me, uncle of Exeter.   180

       [*Gloucester and Warwick hasten after Fluellen;*
          the King, Exeter and the rest following

[4. 8.]   *Before King Henry's pavilion*

    GOWER *and* WILLIAMS *in conversation*

Williams. I warrant it is to knight you, captain.

    FLUELLEN *is seen approaching*

Fluellen. [*hails Gower*] God's will, and his pleasure,
captain, I beseech you now, come apace to the king:
there is more good toward you, peradventure, than is in
your knowledge to dream of. [*Williams confronts him*
  Williams. [*points to his own bonnet*] Sir, know you
this glove?
  Fluellen. Know the glove? I know the glove is a glove.
  Williams. [*points to Fluellen's cap*] I know this, and
    thus I challenge it.   [*'strikes him'* 10

Fluellen. 'Sblood, an arrant traitor as any's in the universal world, or in France, or in England.

Gower. How now, sir? you villain!

Williams. Do you think I'll be forsworn?

Fluellen. Stand away, Captain Gower, I will give treason his payment into plows, I warrant you.

Williams. I am no traitor.

Fluellen. That's a lie in thy throat. I charge you in his majesty's name, apprehend him, he's a friend of the
20 Duke Alençon's.

WARWICK and GLOUCESTER hurry up, with the King and Exeter following

Warwick. How now, how now, what's the matter?

Fluellen. My Lord of Warwick, here is, praised be God for it, a most contagious treason come to light, look you, as you shall desire in a summer's day....Here is his majesty.

King Henry. Now now, what's the matter?

Fluellen. My liege, here is a villain and a traitor, that, look your grace, has struck the glove which your majesty is take out of the helmet of Alençon.

30 *Williams.* My liege, this was my glove, here is the fellow of it: and he that I gave it to in change promised to wear it in his cap: I promised to strike him, if he did: I met this man with my glove in his cap, and I have been as good as my word.

Fluellen. Your majesty, hear now, saving your majesty's manhood, what an arrant, rascally, beggarly, lousy knave it is: I hope your majesty is pear me testimony and witness, and will avouchment, that this is the glove of Alençon, that your majesty is give me, in your conscience now.

40 *King Henry.* Give me thy glove, soldier; look, here is the fellow of it:

'Twas I indeed thou promised'st to strike,
And thou hast given me most bitter terms.

Fluellen. An please your majesty, let his neck answer
for it, if there is any martial law in the world.

King Henry. How canst thou make me satisfaction?

Williams. All offences, my lord, come from the heart:
never came any from mine that might offend your
majesty.

King Henry. It was ourself thou didst abuse.　　50

Williams. Your majesty came not like yourself: you
appeared to me but as a common man; witness the night,
your garments, your lowliness: and what your highness
suffered under that shape, I beseech you take it for your
own fault, and not mine: for had you been as I took you
for, I made no offence; therefore I beseech your highness
pardon me.

King Henry. Here, uncle Exeter, fill this glove
　　with crowns,
And give it to this fellow. Keep it, fellow,
And wear it for an honour in thy cap,　　60
Till I do challenge it. Give him the crowns:
And, captain, you must needs be friends with him.

Fluellen. By this day and this light, the fellow has
mettle enough in his belly... [*takes a shilling from his
poke*] Hold, there is twelve-pence for you, and I pray
you to serve God, and keep you out of prawls and
prabbles, and quarrels and dissensions, and I warrant
you it is the better for you.

Williams. I will none of your money.

Fluellen. It is with a good will: I can tell you it will 70
serve you to mend your shoes: come, wherefore should
you be so pashful? your shoes is not so good: 'tis a good
silling, I warrant you, or I will change it.

An English HERALD returns from the battlefield

King Henry. Now, herald, are the dead numbered?
Herald. Here is the number of the slaughtered French.
          [he delivers a paper
 King Henry. What prisoners of good sort are
  taken, uncle?
 Exeter. Charles Duke of Orleans, nephew to the king,
John Duke of Bourbon, and Lord Bouciqualt:
Of other lords and barons, knights and squires,
80 Full fifteen hundred, besides common men.
 King Henry. This note doth tell me of ten
  thousand French
That in the field lie slain: of princes, in this number,
And nobles bearing banners, there lie dead
One hundred twenty-six: added to these,
Of knights, esquires, and gallant gentlemen,
Eight thousand and four hundred: of the which,
Five hundred were but yesterday dubbed knights.
So that, in these ten thousand they have lost,
There are but sixteen hundred mercenaries:
90 The rest are princes, barons, lords, knights, squires,
And gentlemen of blood and quality.
The names of those their nobles that lie dead:—
Charles Delabreth, high constable of France,
Jaques of Chatillon, admiral of France,
The master of the cross-bows, Lord Rambures,
Great Master of France, the brave
  Sir Guichard Dolphin,
John Duke of Alençon, Anthony Duke of Brabant,
The brother to the Duke of Burgundy,
And Edward Duke of Bar: of lusty earls,
100 Grandpré and Roussi, Faulconbridge and Foix,
Beaumont and Marle, Vaudemont and Lestrake.

Here was a royal fellowship of death!
Where is the number of our English dead?

                 [the herald presents another paper

Edward the Duke of York, the Earl of Suffolk,
Sir Richard Kikely, Davy Gam, esquire;
None else of name: and, of all other men,
But five and twenty....O God, thy arm was here:
And not to us, but to thy arm alone,
Ascribe we all: when, without stratagem,
But in plain shock, and even play of battle,   110
Was ever known so great and little loss,
On one part and on th'other? Take it, God,
For it is none but thine!

  Exeter.   'Tis wonderful!

  King Henry. Come, go we in procession to the village:
And be it death proclaiméd through our host
To boast of this or take that praise from God
Which is his only.

  Fluellen. Is it not lawful, an please your majesty, to
tell how many is killed?

  King Henry. Yes, captain: but with
     this acknowledgement,   120
That God fought for us.

  Fluellen. Yes, my conscience, he did us great good.

  King Henry. Do we all holy rites:
Let there be sung 'Non nobis' and 'Te Deum',
The dead with charity enclosed in clay:
And then to Calais, and to England then,
Where ne'er from France arrived more happy men.

                [they move on towards the village

[5. Prologue]

'*Enter Chorus*'

Chorus. Vouchsafe to those that have not read the story,
That I may prompt them: and of such as have,
I humbly pray them to admit th'excuse
Of time, of numbers, and due course of things,
Which cannot in their huge and proper life
Be here presented....Now we bear the king
Toward Calais: grant him there; there seen,
Heave him away upon your wingéd thoughts,
Athwart the sea: behold the English beach
10 Pales in the flood with men, with wives, and boys,
Whose shouts and claps out-voice the deep-mouthed sea,
Which like a mighty whiffler 'fore the king
Seems to prepare his way: so let him land,
And solemnly see him set on to London.
So swift a pace hath thought, that even now
You may imagine him upon Blackheath:
Where that his lords desire him to have borne
His bruiséd helmet, and his bended sword
Before him through the city: he forbids it,
20 Being free from vainness and self-glorious pride;
Giving full trophy, signal, and ostent,
Quite from himself, to God....But now behold,
In the quick forge and working-house of thought,
How London doth pour out her citizens—
The mayor and all his brethren in best sort,
Like to the senators of th'antique Rome,
With the plebeians swarming at their heels,
Go forth and fetch their conqu'ring Cæsar in:
As, by a lower but loving likelihood,
30 Were now the general of our gracious empress,

As in good time he may, from Ireland coming,
Bringing rebellion broachéd on his sword,
How many would the peaceful city quit,
To welcome him! much more, and much more cause,
Did they this Harry....Now in London place him—
As yet the lamentation of the French
Invites the King of England's stay at home:
The emperor's coming in behalf of France,
To order peace between them—and omit
All the occurrences, whatever chanced,   40
Till Harry's back-return again to France:
There must we bring him; and myself have played
The interim, by rememb'ring you 'tis past.
Then brook abridgement, and your eyes advance,
After your thoughts, straight back again to France.

                           ['*Exit*'

[5. 1.]   *France. The English camp*

    GOWER *and* FLUELLEN (*a leek in his cap and
a cudgel beneath his arm*)

  Gower. Nay, that's right...But why wear you your
leek to-day? Saint Davy's day is past.

  Fluellen. There is occasions and causes why and
wherefore in all things: I will tell you, ass my friend,
Captain Gower; the rascally, scauld, beggarly, lousy,
pragging knave Pistol, which you and yourself, and all
the world, know to be no petter than a fellow, look you
now, of no merits—he is come to me, and prings me
pread and salt yesterday, look you, and bid me eat my
leek: it was in a place where I could not breed no   10
contention with him; but I will be so bold as to wear it
in my cap till I see him once again, and then I will tell
him a little piece of my desires.

PISTOL is seen strutting towards them

Gower. Why, here he comes, swelling like a turkey-cock.

Fluellen. 'Tis no matter for his swellings, nor his turkey-cocks....God pless you, Ancient Pistol! you scurvy lousy knave, God pless you.

Pistol. Ha! art thou bedlam? Dost thou thirst, base Trojan,
20 To have me fold up Parca's fatal web?
Hence! I am qualmish at the smell of leek.

Fluellen. I peseech you heartily, scurvy lousy knave, at my desires, and my requests, and my petitions, to eat, look you, this leek; because, look you, you do not love it, nor your affections, and your appetites and your disgestions does not agree with it, I would desire you to eat it.

Pistol. Not for Cadwallader and all his goats.

Fluellen. There is one goat for you. [*'strikes him'*]
30 Will you be so good, scauld knave, as eat it?

Pistol. Base Trojan, thou shalt die. [*draws his sword*

Fluellen. You say very true, scauld knave, when God's will is: I will desire you to live in the mean time, and eat your victuals: come, there is sauce for it....[*striking him again*] You called me yesterday mountain-squire, but I will make you to-day 'a squire of low degree'.... [*he knocks him down*] I pray you fall to—if you can mock a leek, you can eat a leek.

Gower. Enough, captain, you have astonished him.
40 *Fluellen.* [*kneels upon him*] I say, I will make him eat some part of my leek, or I will peat his pate four days: bite, I pray you, it is good for your green wound, and your ploody coxcomb.

[*he thrusts the leek between his teeth*

Pistol. Must I bite?

Fluellen. Yes certainly, and out of doubt and out of
question too, and ambiguities.   [*he cudgels him*

Pistol. [*roaring in pain*] By this leek, I will most
horribly revenge I eat and eat I swear.

Fluellen. Eat, I pray you, will you have some more
sauce to your leek? there is not enough leek to swear by. 50
                                        [*he beats him again*

Pistol. [*whimpers*] Quiet thy cudgel, thou dost see I eat.

Fluellen. Much good do you, scauld knave, heartily....
[*he releases Pistol*] Nay, pray you throw none away,
the skin is good for your broken coxcomb; when you
take occasions to see leeks hereafter, I pray you mock at
'em, that is all.

Pistol. Good.

Fluellen. Ay, leeks is good...Hold you, there is a groat
to heal your pate.

Pistol. Me a groat!   60

Fluellen. Yes verily, and in truth you shall take it, or
I have another leek in my pocket, which you shall eat.

Pistol. I take thy groat in earnest of revenge.

Fluellen. If I owe you any thing, I will pay you in
cudgels, you shall be a woodmonger, and buy nothing
of me but cudgels...God bye you, and keep you, and
heal your pate.   [*he goes*

Pistol. All hell shall stir for this.

Gower. Go, go, you are a counterfeit cowardly knave—
will you mock at an ancient tradition, began upon an 70
honourable respect, and worn as a memorable trophy of
predeceased valour, and dare not avouch in your deeds
any of your words? I have seen you gleeking and galling
at this gentleman twice or thrice. You thought, because
he could not speak English in the native garb, he could
not therefore handle an English cudgel: you find it

otherwise, and henceforth let a Welsh correction teach
you a good English condition—fare ye well.   [*he goes*
  Pistol. Doth Fortune play the huswife with me now?
80 News have I that †my Doll is dead i'th'spital
   O' malady of France,
And there my rendezvous is quite cut off...
Old I do wax, and from my weary limbs
Honour is cudgelled....Well, bawd I'll turn,
And something lean to cutpurse of quick hand:
To England will I steal, and there I'll steal:
And patches will I get unto these cudgelled scars,
And swear I got them in the Gallia wars.
                        [*he hobbles away*

[5. 2.]   *France. A royal palace*

'*Enter, at one door,* King HENRY, EXETER, BEDFORD,
WARWICK', GLOUCESTER, WESTMORELAND, '*and other
Lords; at another,* Queen ISABEL, *the*' FRENCH 'KING',
the Princess KATHARINE, ALICE, *and other Ladies,* '*the
Duke of* BURGUNDY, *and other French*'

  King Henry. Peace to this meeting, wherefore we
     are met!
Unto our brother France, and to our sister,
Health and fair time of day: joy and good wishes
To our most fair and princely cousin Katharine:
And, as a branch and member of this royalty,
By whom this great assembly is contrived,
We do salute you, Duke of Burgundy;
And, princes French, and peers, health to you all!
  French King. Right joyous are we to behold your face,
10 Most worthy brother England, fairly met—
So are you, princes English, every one.

Qyeen Isabel. So happy be the issue, brother England,
Of this good day, and of this gracious meeting,
As we are now glad to behold your eyes,
Your eyes which hitherto have borne in them
Against the French, that met them in their bent,
The fatal balls of murdering basilisks.
The venom of such looks, we fairly hope,
Have lost their quality, and that this day
Shall change all griefs and quarrels into love.   20
 King Henry. To cry amen to that, thus we appear.
 Qyeen Isabel. You English princes all, I do salute you.
 Burgundy. My duty to you both, on equal love....
Great kings of France and England: that I
  have laboured
With all my wits, my pains, and strong endeavours,
To bring your most imperial majesties
Unto this bar and royal interview,
Your mightiness on both parts best can witness....
Since then my office hath so far prevailed,
That face to face, and royal eye to eye,   30
You have congreeted: let it not disgrace me,
If I demand before this royal view,
What rub, or what impediment there is,
Why that the naked, poor, and mangled Peace,
Dear nurse of arts, plenties, and joyful births,
Should not in this best garden of the world,
Our fertile France, put up her lovely visage?
Alas, she hath from France too long been chased,
And all her husbandry doth lie on heaps,
Corrupting in it own fertility.   40
Her vine, the merry cheerer of the heart,
Unprunéd, dies: her hedges even-pleached,
Like prisoners wildly over-grown with hair,
Put forth disordered twigs: her fallow leas

The darnel, hemlock, and rank fumitory
Doth root upon; while that the coulter rusts,
That should deracinate such savagery:
The even mead, that erst brought sweetly forth
The freckled cowslip, burnet, and green clover,
50 Wanting the scythe, all uncorrected, rank,
Conceives by idleness, and nothing teems
But hateful docks, rough thistles, kecksies, burs,
Losing both beauty and utility;
And as our vineyards, fallows, meads, and hedges,
Defective in their natures, grow to wildness,
Even so our houses, and ourselves, and children,
Have lost, or do not learn, for want of time,
The sciences that should become our country;
But grow like savages, as soldiers will,
60 That nothing do but meditate on blood,
To swearing, and stern looks, diffused attire,
And every thing that seems unnatural.
Which to reduce into our former favour,
You are assembled: and my speech entreats,
That I may know the let, why gentle Peace
Should not expel these inconveniences,
And bless us with her former qualities.
   King Henry. If, Duke of Burgundy, you would
     the peace,
Whose want gives growth to th'imperfections
70 Which you have cited, you must buy that peace
With full accord to all our just demands,
Whose tenours and particular effects
You have, enscheduled briefly, in your hands.
   Burgundy. The king hath heard them: to the which,
     as yet,
There is no answer made.
   King Henry. Well then: the peace, which you
     before so urged,

Lies in his answer.

  French King. I have but with a †cursitory eye
O'erglanced the articles: pleaseth your grace
To appoint some of your council presently   80
To sit with us once more, with better heed
To re-survey them; we will suddenly
Pass our accept and peremptory answer.

  King Henry. Brother, we shall....Go, uncle
      Exeter,
And brother Clarence, and you, brother Gloucester,
Warwick, and Huntingdon, go with the king,
And take with you free power, to ratify,
Augment, or alter, as your wisdoms best
Shall see advantageable for our dignity,
Any thing in or out of our demands,   90
And we'll consign thereto....Will you, fair sister,
Go with the princes, or stay here with us?

  Queen Isabel. Our gracious brother, I will go
      with them:
Haply a woman's voice may do some good,
When articles too nicely urged be stood on.

  King Henry. Yet leave our cousin Katharine here
      with us,
She is our capital demand, comprised
Within the fore-rank of our articles.

  Queen Isabel. She hath good leave.

        [*All depart but King Henry, Katharine,
                     and her Gentlewoman*

  King Henry.   Fair Katharine, and most fair,
Will you vouchsafe to teach a soldier terms,   100
Such as will enter at a lady's ear,
And plead his love-suit to her gentle heart?

  Katharine. Your majesty shall mock at me, I cannot
speak your England.

  King Henry. O fair Katharine, if you will love me

soundly with your French heart, I will be glad to hear
you confess it brokenly with your English tongue. Do
you like me, Kate?

Katharine. Pardonnez moi, I cannot tell vat is 'like
110 me'.

King Henry. An angel is like you, Kate, and you are
like an angel.

Katharine. Que dit-il? que je suis semblable à les
anges?

Alice. Oui, vraiment, sauf votre grace, ainsi dit-il.

King Henry. I said so, dear Katharine, and I must not
blush to affirm it.

Katharine. O bon Dieu! les langues des hommes sont
pleines de tromperies.

120 *King Henry.* What says she, fair one? that the tongues
of men are full of deceits?

Alice. Oui, dat de tongues of de mans is be full of
deceits: dat is de princess.

King Henry. The princess is the better English-
woman…I'faith, Kate, my wooing is fit for thy understanding; I am glad thou canst speak no better English,
for, if thou couldst, thou wouldst find me such a plain
king, that thou wouldst think I had sold my farm to buy
my crown…. I know no ways to mince it in love, but
130 directly to say "I love you"; then if you urge me farther
than to say "Do you in faith?" I wear out my suit…
Give me your answer, i'faith do, and so clap hands,
and a bargain: how say you, lady?

Katharine. Sauf votre honneur, me understand vell.

King Henry. Marry, if you would put me to verses,
or to dance for your sake, Kate, why, you undid me:
for the one, I have neither words nor measure; and for
the other, I have no strength in measure, yet a reasonable
measure in strength. If I could win a lady at leap-frog,

or by vaulting into my saddle with my armour on my 140
back, under the correction of bragging be it spoken,
I should quickly leap into a wife: or if I might buffet
for my love, or bound my horse for her favours, I could
lay on like a butcher, and sit like a jack-an-apes, never
off. But before God, Kate, I cannot look greenly, nor
gasp out my eloquence, nor I have no cunning in pro-
testation; only downright oaths, which I never use till
urged, nor never break for urging. If thou canst love
a fellow of this temper, Kate, whose face is not worth
sun-burning, that never looks in his glass for love of any 150
thing he sees there, let thine eye be thy cook. I speak to
thee plain soldier: if thou canst love me for this, take
me; if not, to say to thee that I shall die is true; but for
thy love, by the Lord, no: yet I love thee too. And
while thou liv'st, dear Kate, take a fellow of plain and
uncoined constancy, for he perforce must do thee right,
because he hath not the gift to woo in other places: for
these fellows of infinite tongue, that can rhyme themselves into ladies' favours, they do always reason themselves out again. What! a speaker is but a prater, a rhyme 160
is but a ballad; a good leg will fall, a straight back will
stoop, a black beard will turn white, a curled pate will
grow bald, a fair face will wither, a full eye will wax
hollow: but a good heart, Kate, is the sun and the moon,
or rather the sun and not the moon; for it shines bright,
and never changes, but keeps his course truly. If thou
would have such a one, take me! And take me, take a
soldier: take a soldier, take a king. And what say'st
thou then to my love? speak, my fair, and fairly, I pray
thee.   170

Katharine. Is it possible dat I sould love de enemy of
France?

King Henry. No, it is not possible you should love the

enemy of France, Kate; but, in loving me, you should
love the friend of France: for I love France so well
that I will not part with a village of it; I will have it all
mine: and, Kate, when France is mine, and I am yours,
then yours is France, and you are mine.

Katharine. I cannot tell vat is dat.

180 *King Henry.* No, Kate? I will tell thee in French,
which I am sure will hang upon my tongue like a
new-married wife about her husband's neck, hardly to
be shook off...Je quand sur le possession de France, et
quand vous avez le possession de moi,—let me see, what
then? Saint Dennis be my speed!—donc votre est France,
et vous êtes mienne. It is as easy for me, Kate, to con-
quer the kingdom, as to speak so much more French:
I shall never move thee in French, unless it be to laugh
at me.

190 *Katharine.* Sauf votre honneur, le Français que vous
parlez, il est meilleur que l'Anglais lequel je parle.

King Henry. No, faith, is't not, Kate: but thy speaking
of my tongue, and I thine, most truly falsely, must needs
be granted to be much at one. But, Kate, dost thou
understand thus much English? Canst thou love me?

Katharine. I cannot tell.

King Henry. Can any of your neighbours tell, Kate?
I'll ask them....Come, I know thou lovest me: and at
night, when you come into your closet, you'll question
200 this gentlewoman about me; and I know, Kate, you will
to her dispraise those parts in me that you love with
your heart: but, good Kate, mock me mercifully, the
rather, gentle princess, because I love thee cruelly. If
ever thou beest mine, Káte, as I have a saving faith
within me tells me thou shalt, I get thee with scambling,
and thou must therefore needs prove a good soldier-
breeder: shall not thou and I, between Saint Dennis and

Saint George, compound a boy, half French half
English, that shall go to Constantinople, and take the
Turk by the beard? shall we not? what say'st thou, my 210
fair flower-de-luce?

Katharine. I do not know dat.

King Henry. No: 'tis hereafter to know, but now to
promise: do but now promise, Kate, you will endeavour
for your French part of such a boy; and, for my English
moiety, take the word of a king and a bachelor. How
answer you, la plus belle Katharine du monde, mon très
cher et devin déesse?

Katharine. Your majestee 'ave fause French enough
to deceive de most sage demoiselle dat is en France.   220

King Henry. Now fie upon my false French! By mine
honour, in true English, I love thee, Kate; by which
honour, I dare not swear thou lovest me, yet my blood
begins to flatter me that thou dost; notwithstanding the
poor and untempering effect of my visage. Now beshrew
my father's ambition! he was thinking of civil wars
when he got me, therefore was I created with a stubborn
outside, with an aspect of iron, that when I come to woo
ladies, I fright them: but in faith, Kate, the elder I wax,
the better I shall appear. My comfort is, that old age, 230
that ill layer up of beauty, can do no more spoil upon
my face. Thou hast me, if thou hast me, at the worst;
and thou shalt wear me, if thou wear me, better and
better: and therefore tell me, most fair Katharine, will
you have me? Put off your maiden blushes, avouch the
thoughts of your heart with the looks of an empress, take
me by the hand, and say "Harry of England, I am
thine": which word thou shalt no sooner bless mine ear
withal, but I will tell thee aloud "England is thine,
Ireland is thine, France is thine, and Henry Plantagenet 240
is thine"; who, though I speak it before his face, if he

be not fellow with the best king, thou shalt find the best king of good fellows....Come, your answer in broken music; for thy voice is music, and thy English broken: therefore, queen of all, Katharine, break thy mind to me in broken English; wilt thou have me?

Katharine. Dat is as it sall please de roi mon père.

King Henry. Nay, it will please him well, Kate; it shall please him, Kate.

250 *Katharine.* Den it sall also content me.

King Henry. Upon that I kiss your hand, and I call you my queen.

Katharine. Laissez, mon seigneur, laissez, laissez: ma foi, je ne veux point que vous abaissiez votre grandeur en baisant la main d'une de votre seigneurie indigne serviteur; excusez-moi, je vous supplie, mon très-puissant seigneur.

King Henry. Then I will kiss your lips, Kate.

Katharine. Les dames et demoiselles pour être baisées 260 devant leur noces, il n'est pas la coutume de France.

King Henry. Madam my interpreter, what says she?

Alice. Dat it is not be de fashon pour les ladies of France,—I cannot tell vat is baiser en Anglish.

King Henry. To kiss.

Alice. Your majestee entendre bettre que moi.

King Henry. It is not a fashion for the maids in France to kiss before they are married, would she say?

Alice. Oui, vraiment.

King Henry. O, Kate, nice customs curtsy to great 270 kings. Dear Kate, you and I cannot be confined within the weak list of a country's fashion: we are the makers of manners, Kate; and the liberty that follows our places stops the mouth of all find-faults, as I will do yours, for upholding the nice fashion of your country, in denying me a kiss: therefore patiently, and yielding. [*kissing her*]

You have witchcraft in your lips, Kate: there is more
eloquence in a sugar touch of them than in the tongues
of the French council; and they should sooner persuade
Harry of England than a general petition of monarchs....
Here comes your father.   280

The FRENCH KING *and* QUEEN *return with* BURGUNDY,
EXETER, WESTMORELAND, *and other French and English
Lords; the ladies talk apart*

Burgundy. God save your majesty! my royal cousin,
teach you our princess English?

King Henry. I would have her learn, my fair cousin,
how perfectly I love her, and that is good English.

Burgundy. Is she not apt?

King Henry. Our tongue is rough, coz, and my condition is not smooth: so that, having neither the voice
nor the heart of flattery about me, I cannot so conjure
up the spirit of love in her, that he will appear in his
true likeness.   290

Burgundy. Pardon the frankness of my mirth, if I
answer you for that. If you would conjure in her, you
must make a circle: if conjure up love in her in his true
likeness, he must appear naked, and blind. Can you
blame her then, being a maid yet rosed over with the
virgin crimson of modesty, if she deny the appearance
of a naked blind boy in her naked seeing self? It were,
my lord, a hard condition for a maid to consign to.

King Henry. Yet they do wink and yield, as love is
blind and enforces.   300

Burgundy. They are then excused, my lord, when they
see not what they do.

King Henry. Then, good my lord, teach your cousin
to consent winking.

Burgundy. I will wink on her to consent, my lord, if

you will teach her to know my meaning: for maids, well summered and warm kept, are like flies at Bartholomew-tide, blind, though they have their eyes, and then they will endure handling, which before would not abide 310 looking on.

King Henry. This moral ties me over to time, and a hot summer; and so I shall catch the fly, your cousin, in the latter end, and she must be blind too.

Burgundy. As love is, my lord, before it loves.

King Henry. It is so: and you may, some of you, thank love for my blindness, who cannot see many a fair French city for one fair French maid that stands in my way.

French King. Yes, my lord, you see them perspectively: 320 the cities turned into a maid; for they are all girdled with maiden walls, that war hath never entered.

King Henry. Shall Kate be my wife?

French King. So please you.

King Henry. I am content, so the maiden cities you talk of may wait on her: so the maid that stood in the way for my wish shall show me the way to my will.

French King. We have consented to all terms of reason.

King Henry. Is't so, my lords of England?

330 *Westmoreland.* The king hath granted every article: His daughter first; and then in sequel all, According to their firm proposéd natures.

Exeter. Only he hath not yet subscribéd this: Where your majesty demands that the King of France, having any occasion to write for matter of grant, shall name your highness in this form, and with this addition, in French: Notre très-cher fils Henri, Roi d'Angleterre, Héritier de France: and thus in Latin; Præclarissimus filius noster Henricus, Rex Angliæ, et hæres Franciæ.

French King. Nor this I have not, brother, so denied, 340
But your request shall make me let it pass.
  King Henry. I pray you then, in love and dear alliance,
Let that one article rank with the rest,
And thereupon give me your daughter.
  French King. Take her, fair son, and from her blood
      raise up
Issue to me, that the contending kingdoms
Of France and England, whose very shores look pale
With envy of each other's happiness,
May cease their hatred; and this dear conjunction
Plant neighbourhood and Christian-like accord   350
In their sweet bosoms: that never war advance
His bleeding sword 'twixt England and fair France.
  All. Amen!
  King Henry Now welcome, Kate: and bear me
      witness all,
That here I kiss her as my sovereign queen.
                       ['*Flourish*'
  Queen Isabel. God, the best maker of all marriages,
Combine your hearts in one, your realms in one!
As man and wife, being two, are one in love,
So be there 'twixt your kingdoms such a spousal,
That never may ill office, or fell jealousy,   360
Which troubles oft the bed of blessèd marriage,
Thrust in between the paction of these kingdoms,
To make divorce of their incorporate league:
That English may as French, French Englishmen,
Receive each other....God speak this Amen!
  All. Amen!
  King Henry. Prepare we for our marriage: on which
      day,
My Lord of Burgundy, we'll take your oath,
And all the peers', for surety of our leagues.

370 Then shall I swear to Kate, and you to me,
   And may our oaths well kept and prosp'rous be!
        [A trumpet sounds as King Henry leads Katharine
                      forth, the rest following in procession

[Epilogue]

'Enter CHORUS'

Chorus. Thus far, with rough and all-unable pen,
   Our bending author hath pursued the story,
In little room confining mighty men,
   Mangling by starts the full course of their glory.
Small time: but, in that small, most greatly lived
   This star of England. Fortune made his sword;
By which the world's best garden he achieved:
   And of it left his son imperial lord.
Henry the Sixth, in infant bands crowned King
10   Of France and England, did this king succeed:
Whose state so many had the managing,
   That they lost France, and made his England bleed:
Which oft our stage hath shown; and, for their sake,
In your fair minds let this acceptance take.   *[Exit*

WORDSWORTH CLASSICS

General Editors: Marcus Clapham and Clive Reynard
Titles in this series

Pride and Prejudice

Wuthering Heights

Alice in Wonderland

Father Brown: Selected Stories

Great Expectations

Tess of the d'Urbervilles

A Portrait of the Artist

Women in Love

Moby Dick

Hamlet

Twelfth Night

Tom Sawyer & Huckleberry Finn

The Last of the Mohicans

Oliver Twist

Romeo and Juliet

The Picture of Dorian Gray

Sense and Sensibility

The Wind in the Willows

Othello

Vanity Fair

Jane Eyre

Tom Jones

Ghost Stories

Julius Caesar

David Copperfield

The Odyssey

Call of the Wild & White Fang

Gulliver's Travels

Emma

The Scarlet Letter

A Midsummer Night's Dream

20,000 Leagues Under the Sea

Mansfield Park

The Adventures of Sherlock Holmes

The Ambassadors

Macbeth

Don Quixote

The Riddle of the Sands

Dracula

A Tale of Two Cities

Northanger Abbey

The Three Musketeers

The Great Gatsby

Richard II

The Moonstone

Robinson Crusoe

Cranford

Sons and Lovers

Lord Jim

Three Men in a Boat

Dubliners

Tales of Mystery and Imagination

Pickwick Papers

Plain Tales from the Hills

Richard III

Frankenstein

Persuasion

Memoirs of a Woman of
Pleasure: Fanny Hill

The Return of Sherlock Holmes

As You Like It

The Merchant of Venice

Dr Jekyll and Mr Hyde

War and Peace

Candide

Shirley

Secret Agent

Far from the Madding Crowd

Lord Arthur Savile's Crime &
Other Stories

The Case-Book of Sherlock
Holmes

The Hunchback of Notre Dame

The Turn of the Screw & The
Aspern Papers

The Complete Stories of Saki

Villette

Moll Flanders

The Mill on the Floss

Antony and Cleopatra

Lorna Doone

The Woman in White

Madame Bovary

The Taming of the Shrew

The Thirty-nine Steps

Hadrian the VII

Bleak House

Troilus and Cressida

The Red Badge of Courage

Nicholas Nickleby

Les Miserables

The Warden

Henry V

Barchester Towers

Around the World in 80 Days &
5 Weeks in a Balloon

To the Lighthouse

The Tenant of Wildfell Hall

North and South

Raffles: The Amateur Cracksman

King Lear

Confessions of an English Opium
Eater

Tender is the Night

The Mayor of Casterbridge

Kim

Crime and Punishment

Diary of a Nobody

Ivanhoe

The Tempest

Distribution

AUSTRALIA, BRUNEI
& MALAYSIA
Treasure Press
22 Salmon Street, Port Melbourne
Vic 3207, Australia
Tel: (03) 646 6716
Fax (03) 646 6925

DENMARK
BOG-FAN
St. Kongensgade 61A
1264 København K

BOGPA SIKA
Industrivej 1, 7120 Vejle Ø

FRANCE
Bookking International
16 Rue des Grands Augustins
75006 Paris

GERMANY, AUSTRIA
& SWITZERLAND
Swan Buch-Marketing GmbH
Goldscheuerstrabe 16
D-7640 Kehl Am Rhein, Germany

GREAT BRITAIN & IRELAND
Wordsworth Editions Ltd
Cumberland House, Crib Street,
Ware, Hertfordshire SG12 9ET

Selecta Books
The Selectabook
Distribution Centre
Folly Road, Roundway, Devizes
Wiltshire SN10 2HR

RUSSIA & CHINA
UPC Consulting
Wolffinite 36
65200 Vaasa
Finland

HOLLAND & BELGIUM
Uitgeverlj en Boekhandel
Van Gennep BV, Spuistraat 283
1012 VR Amsterdam, Holland

INDIA
OM Book Service
1690 First Floor
Nai Sarak, Delhi – 110006
Tel: 3279823-3265303 Fax: 3278091

ITALY
Magis Books
Piazza Della Vittoria l/C
42100 Reggio Emilia
Tel: 0522-452303 Fax: 0522-452845

NEW ZEALAND
Whitcoulls Limited
Private Bag 92098, Auckland

NORTH AMERICA
Universal Sales & Marketing
230 Fifth Avenue, Suite 1212
New York, New York 10001
Fax: 212-481-3534

NORWAY
Norsk Bokimport AS
Bertrand Narvesensvei 2
Postboks 6219, Etterstad, 0602 Oslo

SINGAPORE
Book Station
18 Leo Drive, Singapore
Tel: 4511998 Fax: 4529188

SOUTH AFRICA, ZIMBABWE
CENTRAL & E. AFRICA
Trade Winds Press (Pty) Ltd
P O Box 20194, Durban North 4016

SPAIN
Libreria Ribera
Dr. Areilza No.19, 48011 Bilbao
Tel: 441-87-87 Fax: 441-80-29

SWEDEN
Akademibokhandelsgruppen
Box 21002, 100 31 Stockholm

DIRECT MAIL
Jay Communications Ltd
Redvers House, 13 Fairmile,
Henley-on-Thames
Oxfordshire RG9 2JR
Tel: 0491 572656 Fax: 0491 573590